# ELEVATING WOMEN LEADERS

"*Elevating Women Leaders* is an outstanding guide for women leaders and prospective leaders (and fathers of daughters, men who are not "table-blockers," and men who want to collaborate effectively with women leaders). Through Dr. Perryman's story of her own growth and the growth of her movement, readers see examples of overcoming obstacles and learn how to 'play to win.' This book provides advice and guidance from a tested and resilient leader, whose life reflects her commitment to empowering and lifting so many others while speaking her truth."

**Patricia A. Wise**
*Attorney; professor of law; former member, EEOC Select Task Force on Workplace Harassment*

"The journey toward leadership is not only filled with ups and downs or the typical hills and valleys, but women encounter unusual 'sharks' and are hampered by ineffective colleagues disguised as 'goldfish.' In this groundbreaking book, Dr. Tracee Perryman, a thought leader and successful entrepreneur, guides you into a captivating and mind-provoking strategy toward overcoming barriers. She intellectually lays the groundwork for all the challenges that are often encountered by bold and creative women. She uses her rich experiences to provide step-by-step guidelines on how to understand who you are, what challenges you are encountering, how to identify effective resources, and how you can effectively build your unique brand. She demystifies ways to recognize toxicity and how to address it, while also giving yourself permission to eliminate it from your status. Believing in yourself and the vision you want to accomplish through well-established approaches are offered. Each chapter offers the reader questions for reflection that provide pathways for future planning.

"*Elevating Women Leaders* is an essential read for any woman embarking on a new path toward success, and whether it is a leadership role, a new job, or an entrepreneurial journey, this book will be one that you will keep reading again and again as each chapter indulges you to think differently about the journey."

**Sherine Obare, PhD**
*Dean, Joint School of Nanoscience and Nanoengineering,*
*North Carolina A&T State University, University of North Carolina*
*at Greensboro*

"Your book is a 'just in the nick of time' resource for those of us who have been around for a while and may be changing careers, for those who are new to their career journey, and for those who are happy where they are. Learning how to 'love me as I am' and being okay with areas that are not my strong suit is a gift I am 're-gifting' to myself. Although your audience is women, I feel the need to share your nuggets of truth and advice with my adult daughters *and* sons.

"Thank you for your bravery in saying the hard stuff. Thank you for putting your thoughts and coaching out there for the world to see. And, thank you for showing all women how to just be who they are without guilt or without paying hundreds of dollars for someone to build their brand.

"I am *not* every woman, but I am me. And that's a good thing!"

**Dr. Bonnie Wilson, DHA, MBA, BSN, RN, PCC, NEA-BC**
*President and founder, Xceeding the Mark, LLC*

ELEVATING
WOMEN
LEADERS

TRACEE PERRYMAN, PHD

# ELEVATING WOMEN LEADERS

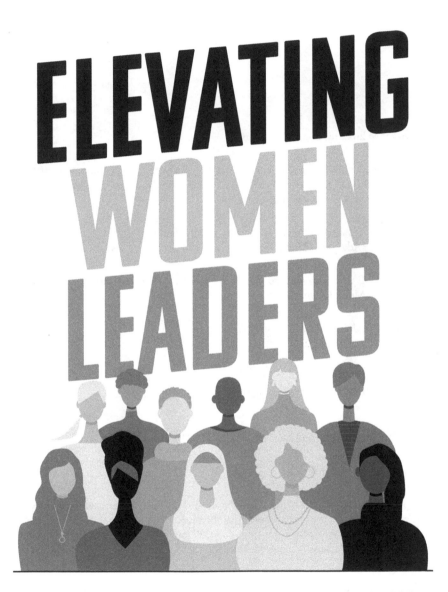

**STORIES OF** STRENGTH, SURVIVAL, AND SUCCESS

*Advantage* | Books

Published by Advantage Books, Charleston, South Carolina.
An imprint of Advantage Media.

ADVANTAGE is a registered trademark, and the Advantage colophon is a trademark of Advantage Media Group, Inc.

Printed in the United States of America.

10 9 8 7 6 5 4 3 2 1

ISBN: 978-1-64225-866-0 (Paperback)
ISBN: 978-1-64225-865-3 (eBook)

Library of Congress Control Number: 2023911631

Cover design by David Taylor.

Advantage Books is an imprint of Advantage Media Group. Advantage Media helps busy entrepreneurs, CEOs, and leaders write and publish a book to grow their business and become the authority in their field. Advantage authors comprise an exclusive community of industry professionals, idea-makers, and thought leaders. For more information go to **advantagemedia.com**.

*I would like to dedicate this book to my parents, Dr. Donald and Willetta. Since a very early age, both gave me the PERMISSION to shine, PERMISSION to be my authentic self, and PERMISSION to blaze my own trail. The wisdoms shared in this book are a reflection of the foundation they laid: to strive for excellence and demonstrate the highest level of ethics.*

*To my niece, Jamison, a rising star in her own right. My goal each day is to work towards creating a world where she does not have to fight to shine.*

*I am because they are!*

# CONTENTS

# *FOREWORD*

When Tracee Perryman asked me to write the foreword for her book, I immediately felt both privileged and honored to do so. When women support women, beautiful things happen. We go against some of the negative messages in our culture that say women are reluctant to support other women. Maybe some are, but that is not me. And that is not Tracee.

Wendy Kurtz of Elizabeth Charles and Associates, LLC, who helped me write and publish my own book (and continues to support me to this day), made the introduction. I was in the middle of getting my daughter ready for high school graduation, selling my home, and moving back to the East Coast. I had every reason to say no. But when life offers you an invitation to support a woman like Tracee, you RSVP quickly and enthusiastically, "Yes!"

Then I opened her book. My eyes widened as they fell upon the chapter subheading, "Answering the Call." I gulped. My heart fluttered. "These are the same words I use to describe why I do what I do in my life," I said silently to myself. These exact words. In addition to being an author, I am a speaker, a leader, and now, a developer of the next generation of leaders for our world. In my former professional life, I answered the call to serve my country as a career naval officer and naval aviator, ultimately retiring as a Navy captain. My new calling is as an educator. For the past two-and-a-half years I have had the privilege to teach leadership to undergraduates at Vanderbilt University.

## WHY THIS BOOK

Women leaders need to be in community with other women leaders. So many times we find ourselves in the minority—either the only woman in the room or one of the only. Leadership can be lonely and as women leaders, perhaps more so. We need to find spaces to be open and honest with each other and share the good, the bad, and the ugly that come with being a woman in leadership. We need each other.

In *Elevating Women Leaders*, Tracee gets radically honest with us and points the way to be honest with ourselves and one another. Her reflection questions are not only inviting, but also piercing in their honesty. When I say piercing, her questions might make you feel just a wee bit uncomfortable—thankfully. Real growth comes from radical honesty.

Tracee is a woman who knows her mission and she excels in it. As she says, "Making a difference in the lives of those without resources and a voice is my call." She lives her call and uses it as a framework for the personal and professional decisions she makes in her life. She doesn't listen to the naysayers in her life. She navigates past them or through them and, as a result, her nonprofit has grown exponentially.

## BRANDING AND BEYOND

Tracee stays true to her brand and teaches us how to do the same. She uses the term "brand" in a most unusual way. You will think differently about your own brand as a result of reading her book. I promise.

Most of us consider our brand as how we present ourselves to the world. Yes, that is true. However, that is only partially true. Tracee extends the concept of branding beyond the external to our internal branding. Sometimes we need to change the stories inside our heads to move forward into our callings. And sometimes we need to take the advice of our mothers (or Tracee's mom at least) to ensure we embrace aesthetics, creativity, and good taste as part of our brand. I smile as I imagine Tracee's mom washing her silver, her hands in warm soapy water, as she passes along her wisdom to her daughter. Woman to woman, the connection matters.

What struck me most profoundly in Tracee's book was the single word PERMISSION. As women, we often use the word *permission* to give unto others. Permission to help others. Permission to put our careers on the back burner. Permission to place ourselves last as the culture often teaches us. Throughout her book, Tracee invites us as women to give ourselves permission in new ways, including permission to walk away, permission to swim with sharks (not the real ones mind you, but others bite nonetheless), and most importantly, permission to be who you are.

I might have read enough about leading with vulnerability and leading with empathy. Yes, it is important that we do so. I wholeheartedly agree. However, we also need to develop, then stand by our brand. We need to lead with PERMISSION. The beauty of *Elevating*

*Women Leaders* is that Tracee shows us HOW to do so. She gives women a hand up, not a handout. Get reading—Tracee gives you permission, and so do I.

**CAPTAIN BARBARA BELL**
EdD, U.S. Navy (ret); Author, *Flight Lessons: Navigating Through Life's Turbulence and Learning to Fly High*

# WHY THIS BOOK, AND WHY NOW?

The year 2022 marked the twenty-fifth anniversary of a mission and movement of which I was a founding member. I began to reflect on this twenty-five-year journey, which started for me as a mentoring program for elementary school–aged girls and a tutoring program for children and youth in grades K–12. All our programming took place in one 12x20 room. There did not seem to be much of a trajectory for the work I was doing. The nonprofit and social service sector in my small Midwestern town was already oversaturated. I was told there already was a nonprofit for every one hundred people.

Much of my journey, particularly the early years, was marked with the word *no*, and doors shut in my face. On other occasions, I was led down roads to nowhere when I encountered those who were too "polite" to say no directly. In other instances, I was told I was flat-out "crazy." Crazy not to utilize my University of Michigan degree to work in the public sector. Crazy not to seek the comfort and stability of a steady job and a doting husband.

Whereas I respect whatever path a woman chooses to take in her life, that path was not for me. I didn't know for sure what I wanted, or how I would achieve what I wanted. But I did know what I didn't want, and that was to be stifled, stuck in a predetermined routine, and told no. I wanted to think outside the box. I wanted to color outside the lines. I wanted to build a family in my time and on my terms. And I didn't care if that required me to spend nearly the first two decades of my adult life *poor*. For me, happiness made me feel rich. Making a difference in the lives of those who could not speak or advocate for themselves was as fulfilling as any external form of validation I could receive. Making a difference in the lives of those without resources and a voice was my call. Equipping others with the skills to also make a difference in the lives of those without resources and a voice was my call. I acknowledged my call. I accepted my call. I answered my call.

> I wanted to think outside the box. I wanted to color outside the lines. I wanted to build a family in my time and on my terms.

So, how did I put myself on the path to fulfilling my call? By reaching back into the principles instilled upon me. At the core of those principles was *permission*. *Permission* to be me, without apology. *Permission* to set my own metrics for success. *Permission* to leverage other external achievements to build and promote my personal brand. PERMISSION to redefine expectations for women leaders. *Permission* to excel. And *permission* to grow.

Now, nearly forty-five years old, with a nonprofit that has grown from a budget of $0 to over $1 million (in an extremely oversaturated market), and also with a nonprofit that has a demonstrated return on investment of $6 for every $1 invested, I have exercised that *permission*. Specifically, *permission* to defy the odds. And getting to this point has been riddled with a number of frustrations, disappointments, struggles, and joys.

Naturally, success is subjective. However, I believe that my journey has taught me some valuable lessons I think women can benefit from—no matter the industry, organization size, and scope of responsibilities. I am sharing pieces of my journey in the hopes we can redefine what it means to be a woman leader. As women, we have led while combatting the pressures to be perfect, excel quietly, be effective but be polite, deliver results without offending anyone, and make contributions without taking credit for them. We must defend against pressures that govern who we are and how we should act, along with direct attacks on our personhoods, our professional achievements, and our abilities to elevate within our respected professions.

I am writing this book because I believe we need a robust, strong group of women who affirm our *permission* to be who we are, define what we want, and achieve what we want. I believe we need a network of women who affirm our permission to acknowledge, accept, and fulfill the calls that each of us is uniquely gifted to achieve. We all have a contribution to make to this world, and it is time we enjoy the journey. Giving ourselves *permission* to exist and excel helps us enjoy our journeys.

In this book, I will tackle five themes of women's leadership.

The first is *Building a Brand, Building a Life*. In this chapter, I discuss self-exploration—figuring out who we are, what we want, and how to pursue what we want without apology. I also discuss how we can balance our career aspirations with our personal desires and goals to create an authentic brand.

The second theme is *Stand by Your Brand*. In this chapter, I present strategies for upholding and defending our ways of being, desires, and paths to our calls when we are challenged by external influences.

The third theme is *Peace While Swimming with Sharks*. In this chapter, I outline a number of tactics that sharks use to distract, discourage, and destroy our calls. I provide strategies for how to navigate those sharks without becoming bitter and resentful.

In the fourth chapter, *Leading with Love*, I continue to build upon how we resist the temptation to become bitter and resentful when we are subject to so many invalidations, attacks, and assaults. I lay out the dividends that leading with love pays and how this way of leading actually yields a number of benefits.

In the fifth and final chapter, *Permission to Fight, Permission to Overcome!*, I discuss the importance of standing our ground. I discuss how we decide when and how to fight. And I emphasize why it is so important to celebrate our achievements and accomplishments.

As you read this book, there will be several places where you can pause to self-reflect about your feelings and experiences. There will be questions that guide you in formulating new strategies for the future. And each chapter will conclude with a challenge to put those new strategies to the test.

Now let us give ourselves permission to read, reflect, reset, restore—and then *overcome!*

# CHAPTER 1

# BUILD A BRAND AND A LIFE

As much as many of us may desire success, how we define success will determine our level of joy and fulfillment. As we seek to define success, and the degree to which our goal is success, we have to first define ourselves. Who are we? Who do we want to be? Are we in touch with what we truly want for ourselves, or are we relying on society or other external voices to determine those definitions for us?

At different phases of my life, defining myself has been easier. What I wanted out of life has always been in the back of my head, but I didn't always feel free to express those wants or pursue them openly. In this chapter, I want to give you permission to define yourself and define your wants for yourself. It is through these definitions that you become intentional in how you present yourself and pursue those wants in a hectic, chaotic world that will quickly co-opt your identity and send you in every direction except the one you want.

I will share some tools as to how we discern our wants from the voices of society and others. I will share my story of how I became in touch with myself outside of my professional identity and work. And in sum, I'll share how I began unapologetically sharing myself—my identity and pursuit of my wants (beyond my work)—and began building my life.

# I'm Not Every Woman: I'm *Me*

As women, we struggle with what is "acceptable" in so many spaces. We struggle with what is acceptable in our peer groups. We struggle with what is acceptable as a mother, sister, cousin, aunt, wife. We struggle with what is acceptable in our professional roles. We struggle with what is acceptable as women in general. We struggle with so many messages from the media, social media, and institutions dictating how we should look, act, interact, and make life choices. During my doctoral studies at Ohio State University, my research further reinforced these realities. Society, media, and culture influence a person's knowledge of available opportunities, their perceptions of what is "normal" to do or achieve, their individual and collective identity, their perceptions of self-efficacy, and ultimately their decisions and behavior.

Here's a story from my childhood that opened my eyes to the reality of such pressures. I remember being about eleven or twelve, but I can't remember the context under which the conversation began. My father used a simple phrase understandable to a pre-teen. "Don't believe what you see on TV."

I also remember being a little older, about fifteen, when we were talking about the culture and dress of the times. I said to my father, "What about Parliament? Didn't they perform on stage in diapers?"

He responded, "But we had sense enough not to walk around in diapers just because the entertainers wore them *while they were performing*! Entertainment is entertainment. It is not meant to educate. We knew not to take entertainers that seriously. Don't believe what you see on TV."

That statement, "Don't believe what you see on TV," prepared me to remain resilient as society, the media, and culture did its best to try to shape Dr. P. During my preteen and teenage years, society or "TV" said, "You must be a size four. Excel, but hide it. Be like a 'cheerleader.' Be bubbly, fluttering like a social butterfly, able to convene a group of friends and admirers."

## I am not quiet, even when my voice is.

If these traits come naturally, then they are to be embraced! But, for me, who had already begun to define and accept myself—then a size ten to twelve—for whom the desire to achieve was innate and uncontainable. For myself, who could never play the middle—either reflective, reserved, and silent, or a force or stance so powerful that the reception was often one of shock or hostility—I had to remember, "Don't believe what you see on TV. Don't buy what they're selling!"

And in taking that wisdom I found that I would *never* align with the societal and media images we commonly see. I am not going to fit all the societal expectations of women. I am not bubbly, and I am not going to hide what I know or apologize for being the source of a contribution. And I am not quiet, even when my voice is. Those societal, media-imposed images do not apply to me. And whether it's okay with anyone else or not, it's okay with me. This exploration and acceptance was the first step in defining myself in the world in which we live, and ultimately beginning to define my brand. I first objectively discovered and accepted who I am *not*. I was able to do so because I was granted *permission* from someone I respected and trusted.

**REFLECTION:** Take this time to explore those traits you know for sure you are *not*.

- What are the things in life that you know you do *not* want?

- Which of these traits and desires do *not* align with societal expectations?

- Which do *not* align with your familial expectations?

- Which do *not* align with the professional expectations of your current employment situation?

Right here, today, I am passing on the *permission* that was granted to me. As a woman. As a unique woman. As a woman with a special, unique call to make a special, unique contribution to this world, I give you *permission* to reject the messages.

Reject the pressure. Reject every expectation not rooted in the care, safety, physical, and emotional wellness of yourself, and anyone trusted in your care. I give you *permission* to reject every message and pressure from any employment situation you find yourself in at this point in your life. I give you *permission* to say, "I may complete this task, but I will not embody these values in my spirit."

*Permission* to not fit the mold, or even agree with the mold, set me on the path to define what it means to be Dr. P. daily, preparing me for the day when the world would tell me over and over, "You don't measure up."

That *permission* also put me on a path to recognize my limitations, without allowing those limitations to negatively impact my defined identity. Some look at my limitations and deem them great, while others look at them and deem them small. But since it's my identity, and thus my story and my brand, I don't worry about how my limitations are perceived or regarded. Instead I cultivate the courage to look my limitations (or perceived limitations) in the eye and accept them. With that permission, I realized that what some called limitations were really differences and not deficiencies at all. I have learned to analyze myself not through someone else's lenses but through my own. Instead of allowing my limitations to reduce my sense of self, I see them as opportunities to grow into the best definition of myself. I see those limitations as opportunities to refine the understanding and presentation of my brand.

## QUESTIONS FOR REFLECTION

- What are your limitations?
- Where do you find most of your limitations manifesting?
- After considering your limitations, what are your opportunities to grow?
- How can you leverage those opportunities without losing your sense of self?

After accepting what I was not as well as my limitations *without* judgment, I was then able to explore and define who I *am*, and how I want to establish myself in this world as "Dr. P."

1. I am loud.
2. I am jubilant.
3. I am energetic.
4. I am tenacious.
5. I am loving.

6.  I am demanding.

7.  I am creative.

8.  I am persistent.

9.  I am strong.

10. I am feminine.

11. I am intense.

12. I am tender hearted.

13. I am God's child.

When I decide whether I want to embark on another personal or professional endeavor or journey, my *yes* is rooted in the acceptance of Dr. P. If I determine any traits that define Dr. P. would be an issue, then I unapologetically say *no*—whether that no is related to participation or acceptance of the current situation.

In our professional spaces, sometimes we do not have the option of saying *no* to those social spaces or activities that challenge, diminish, or attack our brands, or pressure our brands into silence. But remember, even silence is powerful. When you enter a room, you demonstrate your brand if you never say a word. And when you cannot lead with your brand, remember, your confidence speaks volumes. The way you walk, sit, or stand projects your understanding and acceptance of your identity and brand. When you cannot speak about your brand, or highlight it the way you would like, let your presence and confidence speak for you.

## QUESTIONS FOR REFLECTION

Without speaking to what you do or what you prefer, answer the following questions:

- Who are *you*? What are your traits that define you? List enough traits so that someone who knows you would be able to say, that's _____!

- How many people in your life would be able to list the majority of these traits if asked? Are these people who know you personally or professionally? How do they know you? Under what conditions do you interact?

- Based upon your responses, do enough people in your life know the real *you*? Are you leading with your brand? Why or why not?

- What is keeping you from leading with your brand?

I continue to define the true Dr. P.! And you will need to continue to define the true *you*. Then, you will need to become comfortable with the true *you* and become comfortable with making decisions that develop and promote the true *you*. Finally, you will need to become comfortable with amplifying the true *you* and what *you want*.

Defining yourself and what you want will be a necessary building block as you build your brand in the professional space. Most of us will not have access to a branding firm that can do all the work for us. And if you do, that firm will need your input and collaboration to differentiate you in the marketplace. There are some professionals who are gifted enough to create your full brand for you, but many revise and re-create what has already been done. And, often what has already been done rejects the essence of who *we* are!

Therefore, the professionals will need your input to develop a plan rooted in authenticity, which will be necessary for sustainability. We cannot trust or expect others to get into our heads and figure out who we are. And we cannot move with the necessary confidence if we do not know who we are. Finally, we cannot build enthusiasm among stakeholders, team members, and consumers without confidence and authenticity.

## QUESTIONS FOR REFLECTION

- Where do I want to be in the next five, ten, and twenty years? What would I want to see myself doing?

- Who do I have around me that will support the *true me* and where I want to go?

- Do I need more people around me who support me and where I want to go? What kind of people do I need around me to support the real me and where I want to go? And where can I find those people who will support the real me and where I want to go?

- What do I need to start doing now to brand myself so I can attract the people who will support the real me and help me get where I need to go?

I know the journey of self-definition is difficult. It can be even more difficult moving to the next steps, which involve self-acceptance. Self-acceptance requires taking a long, hard look at how we exist and interact in the world around us. We have to realize and accept the consequences that come with an authentically defined woman who makes authentic choices for herself. We have to become intentional about seeking out persons, spaces, and opportunities that align with our personal identities, and who help us find the common ground between our personal and professional identities. It is at that point when we are ready to start figuring out how our personal and professional identities can be intentionally designed to promote our personal and professional brands. But do remember, there are some empowering benefits when we commit to self-definition, increased self-understanding, and propelling our authentic selves into the spotlight.

- We can clearly *articulate* who *we are*.

- We can more quickly determine who will be compatible with and who will be supportive of what *we* want to *do*.

- We can become comfortable with saying, "This is all I got for you. Take it or leave it. Love me or leave me alone."

- We can move on and not look back.

- We can utilize differences (or what some saw as limitations) to stand out in a crowd of conformers.

- We can make those differences work for us.

## CLOSING

After thinking about who you are, what you want, who will support who you are and what you want, and how who you are and what you are helps you build a brand, now let us think about what it means to build a life. We opened with "I am every woman, I am *me*." We explored on a basic level what it means to define ourselves. Now, we will grant ourselves *permission* to exist, without the pressure of a clock dictating when we should make certain moves or achieve certain milestones in our lives. We will grant ourselves *permission* to explore our values, without judgment and without apology, while examining how those values can be woven into helping us build a life and our overall brand.

# Answering the Call

When you freely explore and accept who you are and what you want, you position yourself to answer your call. We give ourselves *permission* to believe that we were not born into this world by mistake and without a unique contribution to make. We are all called to make our own unique contribution. And that contribution is not in relation to how we can serve someone else, though we serve. Our service makes the world brighter by being a blessing to someone else. Our contributions are to be acknowledged and celebrated. But that acknowledgment and celebration starts with *you*!

When you know who you are, what you want, and how you want to present yourself (or your brand) to the world, then you are much less vulnerable to having your call defined for you. I felt from an early age that there was some type of call in my life, but so many times, so many people have tried to define that call for me. I have been labeled an attorney, a politician, a corporate leader, and a preacher. Many may read these comments and say at least these are respectable professions, and in many cases, highly regarded. And that may be true, but they still did not fit. They were not "*my* call."

So, it took decades to figure out what *my* call was supposed to be. I did know in my heart that I was genuinely interested in understanding people—how they thought, why they made particular decisions. I also had a passion for justice and fairness. Initially, I thought the call was to become a journalist. When I graduated from high school, I thought journalism would be the vehicle by which I could advance equity. I thought if people had the right information, they would make equitable decisions. They would influence others to be equitable and kind.

My other passion was attending the University of Michigan. When I enrolled in my first semester, I saw more opportunities in the psychology department. As a matter of fact, psychology classes were the only classes available when it was my turn to enroll as a freshman. So, I decided to try them. I loved psychology classes. I took so many that when it was time to declare a major, the answer was clear and logical in my mind. Finish in psychology and graduate on time.

I also watched one of my psychology professors bring her baby to class in a stroller and teach our section. I thought, "That must be the life for me—spreading knowledge, being attentive to family, and coming to work in a relaxed state of being." However, as graduation neared, I was tired. When I realized the only route to becoming a psychology professor was to apply for a PhD program, which was five more years of schooling, I had had enough.

Instead, I remembered what my father used to always say: "You would make a great businesswoman."

I would tell him, "I was not born to wear navy and gray suits every day. It's not for me."

But then I thought about the earnings, and I compared two years of graduate school to five years in psychology. I tried working on an MBA. The classes that spoke to my enterprising nature did engage me. I did well. I got pretty far in coursework, and then I quit. I was *bored*. Understanding money and how to make money did not interest me unless there was a greater mission tied to the money. And again, conformity is not my thing. The program lost me when the courses failed to speak to my enterprising nature.

So after a nearly five-year break from graduate school, I enrolled in a master's program in mental health counseling. The program fed my desire to understand people. But I didn't see how I could advance equity. I thought there are often greater forces that influence people's decision making, particularly when the decisions do not advance their self-interests. I graduated and knew I would never be a licensed professional counselor.

> **Answering my call gave me validation for all those individuals that questioned my ambition, fortitude, direction, and passion over the years.**

Instead, I moved on to obtain my PhD in social work. Mind you, I graduated fifteen years after obtaining my bachelor's degree. But that social work program is where I finally saw the pieces come together. I saw a path that validated my enterprising nature, with a focus on equity, and a passion for people. That's where I learned I am not an entrepreneur, but a social entrepreneur. It validated my vision for Center of Hope, the nonprofit. It validated all of the years I worked on the nonprofit, while in and out of grad school. It gave me the language to communicate why I spent all those years underemployed. It gave me validation for all those individuals that questioned my ambition, fortitude, direction, and passion over the years. Here are some steps that may help you as you answer *your call*:

1.  Becoming comfortable with the reality that there is a call, and that call can only be answered by *you*.

2.  Accepting that the call would become clearer with time, as long as you remain committed to steps that align with your personal identity, wants, and goals.

3.  Setting up your life in a way where you can hear the call and its nuances and be prepared to carry out the call in its fullness.

## QUESTIONS FOR REFLECTION

1.  What do you love to do? What activities excite you so much that you can't wait to get out of bed in the morning to do them? What would you do every day for free?

2.  What activities do you excel in?

3.  What do you feel you are uniquely called to do in this world? If you don't know or don't know *yet*, what barriers may be keeping you from figuring it out?

4.  What steps can you take to transform those things you love and excel at into an activity that fulfills your call?

## CLOSING

As you ponder on your call—what it is, what about it resonates with you, and how to fulfill that call, stay encouraged! These revelations do not come overnight. Instead, this section was designed to affirm us in our ability to determine, define, and walk in our calls. As you move forward, understand that your call will become clearer. Continue to make positive steps in a direction that affirms your authentic self.

# Stop Trying to Play Catch-Up and Live *Now!*

Many times, I chat with women who feel they are not where they should be at a particular moment in their lives. Sometimes they know what their call is, but they do not feel they are making the appropriate progress. They are frustrated because they are not further along, and they beat themselves up. I can feel the insecurities, frustration, and sense of unworthiness in their voices, because they are measuring themselves by a subjective and often superficial marker. Or they are wearing themselves out trying to play catch-up. It is almost like many of us go through life feeling like we're being chased—to the degree where we don't enjoy earning and receiving our achievements, or just living life in general.

Short story: I want to share an excerpt from an interview with my mother for the Women's Empowerment Project that our nonprofit Center of Hope hosted in early 2020. When asked what advice she would give to the next generation of women leaders, she said, "Don't wait until you achieve a certain status, or a certain position, or you have a certain amount of money—live *now*."

There is so much liberating encouragement in that statement. The statement is full of underlying principles that can help us all live a more liberated life.

1. *My self-worth is not linked to my career or title.* I often observe broken women expecting to receive validation and wholeness from broken organizations and systems. Whereas we should embrace and pursue our professional endeavors, you can live *now* by making the best of your work environment. Find ways to create projects that inspire *you*, even if nobody ever acknowledges your efforts. Oftentimes to position yourself to achieve in your professional life, you still need to be able to engage in broad, meaningful conversations beyond the promotion or marker of success you want.

2. *My self-worth is not linked to what I own.* But I can be strategic in what I purchase. I can transform the things I own into things that inspire and affirm me.

The media and society's preoccupation with wealth has begun to permeate too many conversations, leaving many professionals feeling obligated to purchase assets beyond their wishes or beyond their means. Oftentimes those who work hard and have been compensated appropriately for their skills, expertise, and experience are judged when they do not readily purchase predetermined status symbols that their coworkers, and even authority figures, deem adequate.

This can be a very dangerous cycle if one falls into the trap of engaging in long-term debt because of the pressure of others. In many cases, it makes us beholden to the employment situation we are currently in. Whereas we may love particular status symbols, we must be very careful not to purchase our way into situations where we cannot say *no* or stand on our ethical principles.

Mom also taught me very early that a house is not a home. She taught me how to use that same sense of creativity and good taste in my home décor. She would remind me that size and architecture are great, but they are the start. It is up to the owner to transform a house into a home that is beautiful, captures memories, and stimulates thought and discussion. She would always say, "When you upgrade, you need to have beautiful furniture and accessories to take with you."

Her wisdom taught me how to take modest means and transform them so they're worth more than when I started. She taught me how to transform possessions into "investments" that fulfill me along the way.

I have very early memories of my mother polishing crystal and brass, preparing for one of my father's corporate entertaining events. I would watch her as she would fill the kitchen sink with water and cleaning products. Then she would dunk each item in the sink, wipe it if needed, and then set them on the counter on top of a towel. At the end, she would dry each piece.

My mom would tell you that I was good for conversation but not much good for working. But there was always something about that sparkling crystal and the rainbows I'd see in the sun reflections that captivated me. It made me feel good on the inside. The smell of the products my mother would use also made me feel good.

I remember looking at the walls, full of color. Vibrant colors. Warm colors. Colors that were stimulating. Colors that made me wake up. Want to think. Want to create something. Those colors were complemented by white furniture and white carpet. The white gave the walls grounding and made me feel at peace. At holiday time, you could expect a winter wonderland! Various trees decorated with a consistent theme but each having its own special flair. Garlands above the windows and doors to carry the theme throughout the home. The décor signaled that the holidays were a time for joy.

But aesthetics did not end with crystal, brass, pretty walls and furniture, and holiday décor, though they all are beautiful. As long as I can remember, both of my parents covered the walls of our home with artists, musicians, thinkers, leaders, and everyday folks who looked exactly like me. The décor of my childhood home was a story in and of itself. People singing, people struggling to make ends meet, but people achieving excellence! Those events were not necessarily in my consciousness at the time, but they impacted me in a profound way. A warm, beautiful, clean home that changed with the seasons inspired creativity within me.

I was given *permission* to buy what I *like*. And I used these early principles to transform homes and offices into spaces that edified my spirit. I learned how to be in touch with how I felt, and how my environment impacted how I felt. It taught me how to make my personal space mine, and how to transform my personal space into an area that drew the best out of me. I explored my emotions and my preferences until I found out how different colors speak to me. To this day, I select colors in my home and office that inspire me to think—that inspire me to write, that inspire me to keep going. I learned how to wear my feelings on my walls and not necessarily on my sleeve. I learned how to understand and recognize my moods. I learned to go with the flow of my moods and feelings rather than fight against them. I discovered which colors gave me calm. I discovered which colors inspired me. I discovered which colors made me creative.

But I also learned how to affirm my identity within my home and office spaces. My home is filled with pictures and images that affirm my values. Images with connections between struggle, success, and togetherness. Women operating in their gifts and abilities. Female strength. Females who are full of energy and vitality. Strong families. Images of learning. Images of music. I also display my accomplishments proudly and pictures of myself through the house that represent times when I experienced joy, strength, creativity, and vitality.

On those hard days when I feel like I got nowhere, I can look to my walls and see myself as beautiful. Myself as creative. Myself as inspirational. Myself as a warrior. These images affirm me going out the door in the morning by saying, "Yes you can." "You are enough." "You are not alone." And when I come home, these same images and colors affirm me by saying, "You did," and if I didn't today, "You will" and "You are still enough."

I brought the same principles into my office spaces—offering symbols of strength and resilience to every person who might walk through our doors. I display the organization's accomplishments with many, many framed articles of our clients accomplishing life goals. We are careful to choose colors that are soothing but also communicate a sense of warmth, community, and belonging. We make our spaces comfortable to let our clients and visitors know, "You are welcome here. You are wanted here. We made great efforts to prepare for your arrival." We want visitors to believe, "Yes you can," "You are enough," "You are not alone."

These strategies helped me better enjoy the spaces I occupy while being inspired by the spaces I occupy. They mentally and emotionally prepare me to break barriers and lead change. They help me build a life for myself. It is an exercise in giving myself *permission* to value what I want to value, regardless of what society says women should value. It gives us *permission* to focus *inward*, working on *ourselves*, and what *we* want, so we do not fall into the trap of constant comparison, insecurity, and jealousy. It is an exercise in giving us *permission* to run our races at our pace and to value what we want to value without apology.

But this exercise also gave me *permission* to build a life within my professional space. It allows me to bring the real Dr. P. to every space of my life—home to the world. As a result, when people come to my home or even my office, they often say, "We know whose office or whose house this is!"

Through making the spaces I occupied personal, it gave me roots. I don't feel as if I'm a temporary traveler in my own home or in my place of work.

But at the same time, making those spaces personal propelled my brand as well. An understanding and appreciation of aesthetics, as well as hospitality, can very well come in handy as you build the relationships necessary to grow your network and/or your business. A broad understanding also makes for good, well-rounded conversation, which can move you closer to your personal and/or professional goals. And when you put your personal attention and style into your space, it furthers your brand even more because it's authentic. As a result, people have also begun to accept that I am not my career. I am not my title. And I bring Dr. P. to everything I do. It puts me closer to attracting those who are comfortable with Dr. P., which places me one step closer to unifying with those who are willing to support and help me advance my mission.

## QUESTIONS FOR REFLECTION

1. Take a minute and think about your personal spaces (your home, your office). If you took your personal pictures, name plates, or degrees down, would anyone know it's your home or your office? Why or why not?

2. Think about colors for a moment. What colors excite you? Which calm you? Which motivate you to persist? Which colors make you create or think? What areas of your home would you want to calm you, motivate you, excite you, or inspire you to create?

3. In your office (home or professional), what mood do you prefer? Which colors evoke that mood? If you are unable to paint your walls, what types of accessories could you include to introduce those colors to the space?

4. Is your home space and/or your professional space as personal as you would like? If not, why are you not bringing your personal identity to your home and/or professional space? What is standing in your way?

5. How might personalizing your home and/or office bring more life to your daily routines?

6. How can personalizing your home and/or office help you build your brand? And how might refining that brand help

you in advancing personal and professional relationships that advance your personal mission/goals?

For those who may not have as much comfortability with identifying and using colors, the internet has resources that will tell you what colors evoke which emotions. There are many master classes on design that can show you how to set up a space that will promote your brand within professional guidelines. I also recognize that transforming a space makes a bold statement. It may be a challenge to "step out." But it is also an exercise in developing the boldness and creativity necessary to lead and make a difference.

7. *My self-worth is not linked to my marital status.* After my college years came and went, whispers of "When is she going to get married?" came, followed by the intrusive questions of "When are you going to start your family?" In most cases, these questions were not malicious. They were a manifestation of the natural order of events expected by mainstream society, without consideration for the many complexities that individuals in the twenty-first century face. Over the years, I've learned that "seeming odd" is often a cost of the success we want to see. And for me, now well into my forties, I still have not hit those relational milestones society often expects. I have been married and divorced, but may never experience carrying a child to term, or mothering, period. I have had to accept that some opportunity windows will close as a result of me answering the call to lead.

Many would say I've always been choosy, but I'm much choosier now. I am choosy because I was given *permission* to be choosy. From an early age, I was taught to say *no* to any relationship that was not edifying to my spirit. I was given *permission* to not waste my time in any relationship or arrangement that takes more than it gives. That *permission* gave me the confidence to walk away when necessary, and to stop a train wreck before it gets started. My mother would always say, "Let *no one* treat you like a mule."

Through that lens, I was able to recognize our relationships at home can either give us the energy to take our life's call to the next level. Or our home relationships can suck the energy right out of us—leaving us grieving about opportunities left unexplored and milestones unattained. Seeing how distractions from our relationships can either increase or plummet the altitude of our marks in this world, I became unapologetic about voicing my terms for relationships.

My personal relationships, and particularly romantic relationships, *must* be rooted in

1. mutual respect for one another as people

2. mutual respect for each partner's profession

3. mutual respect for each partner's contributions

4. mutual love and caring for one another

5. mutual commitment to continuous personal growth

6. mutual commitment to the relationship

7. honesty and authenticity

8. love and respect for God

9. mutual commitment to living with integrity

## QUESTIONS FOR REFLECTION

1. Name your five closest relationships. Why did you select them as your closest relationships? Are they family, friends, significant others, or professional relationships?

2. For each relationship you have listed, how does each edify you? How does each help you advance your mission or life goals? How does each help you build a life for yourself?

3. Are there any relationships that do not edify you or not edify you as much as you would like? Why is that? Why did you still list them as one of your closest relationships?

4. In what ways would you expect a significant other to help you advance your personal/professional goals? In what ways would you expect them to help you build a life?

5. What are your criteria for selecting a significant other and life partner? Do you strictly follow those guidelines? Why or why not?

## CLOSING

When we give ourselves *permission* to be choosy, we speak liberation into our spirits rather than words of domination, aggression, and oppression. Granting yourself such *permission* gives you the confidence and inner light to make your mission or life goals a reality.

# The Sassy CEO

Another pressure I have felt over the years is related to personal style. Yes, I am well aware of what constitutes professional attire, and the general expectations for an organizational climate. As I stated before, appreciating aesthetics has been shunned in many environments, and has been used as a reason to dismiss the abilities of women leaders. We have also had to contend with the issue of time and cost. As women, we balance multiple roles in the workplace, our homes, and our communities. We grapple with how to approach looking our best with the limited time we have, and sometimes limited funds.

However, standards for workplace attire are indeed evolving, which present many opportunities for women leaders. Individual expression in appearance is more socially acceptable, which allows us, if done carefully, to use fashion to forward both our personal and professional brands. I am going to share some wisdom my mother shared with me and some strategies I developed on my own to bring a fashion-forward approach to my leadership.

The first tip impressed on me in my early years was *preparedness*. We must be intentional in planning for outfits, as we are intentional in planning other parts of our professional day. My mother used to use Saturdays to wash/dry/press and Sundays to pull out the outfits for the upcoming week. At the very minimum, she pulled out her outfits the night before. There was never any planning for clothes in the morning. I still engage in this routine. I noticed how much time and frustration it has saved me. When I wake up, I can start my day, rather than preparing for my day. If an unexpected situation occurs, I am much less rattled.

For the sake of time, I learned to buy complimentary colors that mix and match well but can also be laundered together. That saves me the time of multiple loads of clothes with multiple care/handling instructions. I typically buy cool-colored jewel tones, so I can wear them in multiple seasons. I also learned to purchase materials that wash easily and dry without wrinkles. That has limited the amount of pressing I need to do. When money permits, I have my clothes dry cleaned. I also take off my clothes as soon as I get home each day to minimize wear and tear.

The second tip I will share is to lead with fashion and not with labels. She taught me how to use fashion as a vehicle of creativity and expression. When we would purchase an upscale accessory, she would say, "That's nice, but how do you plan to build the rest of the look? You still have to do the work." She would also say, "Only buy the item if you would still buy the item without the label. Then you know you're buying because *you* truly like it, and because it's truly high quality." Through that lens, I learned that I did not need to be rich to look good.

Instead, she taught me that when you operate in good taste, you can enter *any* space with confidence. Validating creativity over cost gave me the confidence to explore my personal style and refine it.

The third tip impressed upon me was polish. My mother would always say, particularly for the busy woman, "Keep it simple and polished." Where possible, I wear single pieces so as to not need to match tops and bottoms. I wear dresses underneath blazers, to minimize the number of pieces as well. With my hair, I tend to select styles that stand out, without being fussy. If I have on an outfit in a highly noticeable color or design, then smooth hair works very nicely. And frankly, I don't have time for full makeup all the time. But I do use foundation and a gloss to make sure I have polish and to keep the oil on my face in check. For those days I don't have the time or desire to wear foundation, I rely on a good skin regimen to show the same polish. I am intentional about sending a message that I am conscientious about how I treat myself. I expect you to be conscientious in how you treat me as well.

## QUESTIONS FOR REFLECTION

1. What do you want people to notice about you when you enter a room? How are you conveying that message currently?

2. How do you feel about fashion in general? What or who has influenced your feelings?

3. Is fashion important to you? Whether you answered yes or no, how might you use fashion to promote your overall personal and professional brand? How might you use fashion to convey that message you indicated in question one?

## CLOSING

As you think about your attitudes and values related to fashion, weigh carefully to what degree those attitudes and values may have been shaped by the media, society, or those around you. Are your attitudes and values based on meeting-imposed beauty standards, or are your attitudes/values in rejection of those standards?

The key to branding is being authentic, yet open to other ideas/resources available. Remember, the use of presentation can be leveraged to convey how we want to be addressed, respected, and compensated. It is helpful to find that balance between comfort, convenience, accessibility, and standing out. To lead, we must find ways to distinguish and differentiate ourselves. And, when we can show that we take our personhood seriously, we can leverage a nonverbal opportunity to communicate the same. We are serious about ourselves. We think highly of ourselves. We think highly of our brands. We expect you to do the same.

As you leave this chapter, remember we have the greatest chance of living in freedom, peace, and joy when we are authentic. We become authentic when we take the steps to explore who we are and what we truly value. We then find ways to introduce our whole selves where we have the authority and find strategic ways to let our light shine through in those settings where we have less control.

Please leave this chapter giving yourself *permission* to build a life outside of your career. Then let that life shine through to contribute something new and unique to our world. Lead with *you*. *You* are the brand, and *you* are the *change*. Bring yourself, light, and life to your professional spaces. *They* need *you*!

# Building a Life, Balancing Family, and Dealing with Detours

Two pieces of wisdom I learned from my mother were the importance of family and the importance of making sure our zeal to fulfill our call does not help us lose perspective on ourselves, our homes, our families, and our mortality. My mother's words and actions would always say, "Let nothing outside your household cause you to lose focus on what is going on inside your household."

One of the most painful years of my life was probably 2022. I mourned the loss of my grandmother. Oh, how I loved to see her bright, beautiful smile and hear her sweet laugh. She paid close attention to people and was always so tickled by me. Grandma was obviously from a different generation, where you worked your shift and you went home. Work-life balance and boundaries were more distinct and clearer. For years, she chastised me for what she deemed to be my failure to develop a work-life balance most of my adult life.

My work schedule frankly did not line up with her sleep schedule, so I could not visit her as much as I would have liked.

I eventually bought her an iPad so she could FaceTime me on my lunch break. She would video call several times a week to check on me. She would ask my mom, "How's my baby? She's going to work her little self to death." But over the past year, being able to watch me on video navigate a full day, she began to understand, and our relationship became so much deeper. Just like when I was a little girl, she respected and regarded my gifts and talents but felt a need to protect my kind heart and general positive disposition.

About six months in, my grandmother informed us that her white blood cell count was unusually high. This came as such a shock as only a few weeks earlier, she had been given a clean bill of health from her doctor. She was supposed to go back for more tests to determine if there were any malignancies. I googled every possible explanation for high white blood cell counts. Some were manageable, while others were deadly. I rushed to make improvements to her home that would make her more comfortable and make her feel loved. She said she didn't care if she didn't get to live but one day with the improvements, it would be worth it.

And over the next couple of months, my grandma declined rapidly. When she was admitted to hospitals and rehabilitation facilities, she shared things about her care and lack of care that she was not safe to disclose in her own home. And none of the paid facilities gave her the care I deemed acceptable either. It broke my heart! I re-evaluated my work-life balance immediately. I could not let my grandma leave this world without care that affirmed her dignity and worth.

Grandma was my "Queen Freddie." I had a hard time leaving her alone. My emotions and sense of mission were in conflict. Building a life and building my mission/brand were somewhat in conflict. I could not move forward, trailblazing at the pace I normally could. I could not "appear" to be the first one to enter the space and the last one to leave. I had to reconfigure how Dr. P. would continue to lead change in her new normal. How would Dr. P. stay on top of threats and keep her mission from falling to pieces while she attended to one of the most important people in her life?

I created "satellite offices" in hospitals, rehabilitation centers, and even hospice, so I could treasure every precious moment left. I managed to work around her naps and shift my breaks to times when I could plug in and hear the things she needed to tell me. When you do not have a medical power of attorney, you are not in position to always demand what needs to be done. So I filled in the gaps of self-care practices that made my grandma feel like "Queen Freddie."

I am so grateful I got the opportunity to do some of the things for her that she had done for me in my life. It was a privilege to care for her, nurture her, speak encouragement to her, sing to her, and just be there. I am thankful she granted me the privilege of bonding with her so closely. I am honored she allowed me to care for her in a very personal way.

Though I came to see her seven days a week, those visits probably did much more for me than they did for her. I witnessed her strength. I heard her pray. I watched her offer praise and thanksgiving in the middle of suffering. I listened to her wisdom. I felt her warmth.

And then, eight months after her passing, I was faced with another life-threatening situation in my family. An extremely competent doctor told my father he had to have surgery, and he needed to have the surgery soon. My father's thyroid had grown to the point where it was restricting both his breathing and ability to safely eat. He was labeled high risk on multiple levels. His surgery lasted nearly three times the normal duration, and his thyroid was twenty times the normal size. He lost a lot of blood during the surgery and was held overnight for observation.

A couple of days after release, my father's blood pressure dropped so low that his organs almost shut down. He was rushed to the emergency room and placed in intensive care. My mother and I watched as doctors and nurses looked with dismay and bewilderment. They could not explain the complications and really did not know if he would ever recover. As soon as he showed signs of recovery, they moved him to a regular room, only for him to experience another relapse. I could see the nurses giving up on my father, but my mother and I were determined that we would not give up. We were determined to ensure my father was treated and cared for as if he had hope of recovery. Our words landed on deaf ears more times than one would believe. So, my father found himself with a roommate. I spent every night in his room for seven days. I slept no more than three hours a night and went to work every day. My mother and other family members relieved me during the day and early evenings. And my father recovered! Medical staff swore he would need months of rehab. He was released after fourteen days and is doing much better.

Those moments were some of the most painful and scariest moments of my life! But, in those moments, I recognized more clearly that I am not my job. Had I not taken the time to focus on family, I would have missed critical time, critical bonding, and critical life lessons. Had I not taken the time to focus

**I recognized clearly that I am not my job. Had I not taken the time to focus on family, I would have missed critical time, bonding, and life lessons.**

on family, my father might not be living today! I also would have missed critical experiences that made Dr. P. a more aware, grounded, intuitive, tender, and strong person! Coming through such devastation and trying to pick up all the pieces on multiple levels at multiple times taught me more about what it means to lead than many of our commonly accepted methods of character building and training.

## QUESTIONS FOR REFLECTION

1. Think about those moments in your life that left your heart wounded. Without justifying or rationalizing unfair or unjust behaviors directed toward you, what strengths did you observe about yourself that you didn't realize you had?

2. What nonprofessional value is most important to you? How did you make that determination?

3. Think about those moments when you had to make tough choices about balancing your life mission with family or other personal value demands. How did you make your choices? How did you leverage common skills, strengths, and resources that could be used to meet needs on both levels?

4. How can the strengths you uncovered and lessons you learned about yourself in balancing life, family, and tragedy advance your brand and help you build your life going forward?

## CLOSING

The strength I learned from supporting my grandma during her life's transition built my brand on such a deeper level. It is amazing to develop strengths in the context of advancing your personal and professional pursuits, but as a leader, it is empowering to those who follow you, when you can also apply those strengths to help/support others.

Reflecting on past challenges and tragedies can also serve as a source of inspiration when you face the next challenge. But they also can remind you of your true values and priorities. I always believed family was important, but going through this transition with my grandma and another health scare with my father are strong reminders to *never* let those I love fall out of focus when I continue to work toward my mission and my call. Those we love and value keep us grounded and moving toward the big picture. It is not enough to build a brand or build a career. We must build a full and holistic life for the day when our professional missions are complete.

# Key Points to Remember

- Building a life requires an understanding and appreciation of oneself, goals, and values.

- We build our brand to define ourselves, so we walk in our path and walk in our call. If we do not properly define ourselves, then our path will be defined for us.

- We are not our careers, nor any external measure of success. It is equally important to affirm and nurture those areas of our personalities, as well as the people around us who do not directly tie to those external factors.

- The road of life will get bumpy! That authentic sense of self will be invaluable when life throws situations at us that challenge all those external measures we worked so hard to build.

# Elevation in Action

After this section I leave you with a few challenges that reinforce our *permission* to build our brands and lives as *we see fit*.

1. Write down ten characteristics about yourself that are non-negotiable. In other words, ten things you refuse to change about yourself. Have you ever been asked to change those things about yourself?

2. For those characteristics you have been asked to change about yourself, after reading this chapter, how will you respond? How will you define and defend your brand?

3. Write down how those characteristics can be leveraged to build and promote your personal brand? What areas might need to be refined from *your* personal assessment? How can you go about refining them?

4. Name five ways you will expand your personal brand to demonstrate the aspects of yourself that do not directly tie to your career? How can these aspects be leveraged to also support your career aspirations?

5. What is your call? How are you leveraging your strengths to advance your call?

# CHAPTER 2

# STAND BY YOUR BRAND!

When you give yourself *permission* to unveil and walk in your brand, expect to be challenged. I have had people challenge my name, integrity, sense of style, competence, and just about everything else you can think of. It comes with the territory. We now live in a society where information is widely accessible. People see you and believe they have personal access to you. They feel comfortable with questioning, challenging, and insulting you. They feel they are entitled to become familiar with every personal aspect and detail of your life.

> Positive people are not always vocal, but know you are inspiring many if you're doing something positive. Even if you don't hear it often.

But believe this—what is negative can be reframed for the positive. Don't forget there are positive people still out there, rooting for you. Positive people are not always vocal. They often use social media and other platforms in a totally different way. But know you are inspiring many if you're doing something positive. Even if you do not hear it very often.

In the society we live in, we have to lean into our strength and stand by our brand!

# You Just Ain't for Everybody!

Have you ever entered a space and noticed that merely existing rattled the nerves of others around you? Have you ever encountered rolled eyes, clicked teeth, stale faces, people turning their backs to you to avoid speaking? Have you ever heard the groans when you speak, or have you ever encountered being interrupted as if the person could not stand the sound of your voice? Have you ever been in a room and made tremendous contributions, only for those contributions to be ignored, challenged, or attributed to every other person and factor other than the contributor?

Well, I have experienced all those things. I have included this discussion here because it can be difficult to build a brand when we feel it is being rejected on arrival. In the earlier stages of my journey, I ignored the overt and covert rejections. Completely.

But as the years went on, I found myself withdrawing altogether from social and professional spaces. Even when I was present physically, I checked out mentally and emotionally. I asked myself, "Why bother?" Eventually, I realized those gestures were designed to chase me out of spaces that could get me closer to meeting the people who could help me advance my mission and carry out my call.

Now, there are still times when engagement is simply not worth it. But you can become more strategic about such engagement. You can handle yourself without concern for the hatefulness of those whose intentions are to distract, detract, and destroy. We must give ourselves *permission* to accept "I ain't for everybody." For somebody we will always be

- Too loud
- Too gregarious
- Too animated
- Too confident
- Too analytical
- Too introspective
- Too creative
- Too bold
- Too colorful
- Too focused
- Too justice minded
- Too vain

- Too quick
- Too complicated
- Too unattractive
- Too busy
- Too goals oriented
- Too lazy
- Too calculating
- Too attention seeking
- Too happy being by herself
- Too bossy
- Too … something!

Most of us women echo at least some or most of these sentiments. We live in a society where we're either too big or too small. We're too loud or too quiet. We're too calculating or too emotional. We're too bossy or too afraid to lead. We're too preoccupied with our appearances or maintaining our homes, or too lazy to maintain our appearances or homes.

Here is one of the ways you can walk into rooms so unconcerned about the unfounded criticism and nasty sneers. I've adopted this mantra: get with it, get over it, or get out of my way! Get with my personality. Get with my talent. Get with my appearance. Get with my way of being. Or get over my personality, talent, appearance, worldview, and way of being. Or get out of my way!

When we say "get out of my way," we give our minds permission to push their foolishness to a part of our brains that we don't nurse. When you've answered your call, and you've got a mission to fulfill, you ain't for everybody. You just ain't for everybody. And that's alright!

We give you *permission* to accept "I ain't for everybody."

## QUESTIONS FOR REFLECTION

1. Are there spaces in your life where you feel rejected? What spaces are they?

2. Why are you interacting in spaces where you feel this rejected? Are they advancing your personal/professional missions? Or are they required?

3. How can *you* communicate, verbally and nonverbally, "Get with it, get over it, or get out of the way!"?

4. What might hold you back from communicating "get with it, get over it, or get out of the way"?

5. How can you feel more comfortable or be more strategic in communicating "get with it, get over it, or get out of the way"?

## CLOSING

Women—rejection is likely inevitable, particularly in a professional space. So often we are forced to work with people with conflicting worldviews, conflicting goals, conflicting values, and conflicting methods of communication. We are impacted by societal expectations to different degrees. But today, we are giving ourselves *permission* to accept ourselves and to exist. We understand we operate in a world that often does not support us or affirm us. But as women, we are creative, intentional, and have the ability to demonstrate ingenuity. We are able to build up the areas of our lives that we can control.

# It's Your Picture: Color Outside the Lines

As we've discussed, as women, we feel like we're in a constant battle against forces setting the lines for us. As research suggests, it is natural for people to immediately and intrinsically place others in categories.[1] The use of categories, to some degree, helps us process the overwhelming amount of information we receive in a day. As we've also discussed, the problem is those lines/categories are often suggested to us by the culture of the times.[2] The culture of the times has not historically been open to capturing the full essence of women. The "lines" have been historically stifling. As the *Harvard Business Review* notes, how we define the lines has tremendous consequences when

---

1    Adam Alter, "Why It's Dangerous to Label People," *Psychology Today*, May 2010, accessed May 17, 2023, https://www.psychologytoday.com/us/blog/alternative-truths/201005/why-its-dangerous-label-people.

2    Ibid.

managers make decisions.[3] As women, we are often impacted by those decisions because we are often those who do not make the "cut." When the lines are drawn, we are often left on the outside, looking in.

I have wrestled with this issue for so many years, particularly in the professional space. There has been a particular image of how women in authority should act. In business, linear thinking has been encouraged and embraced. I did and have not seen room for creatives in the heralded narrative of leadership. There I was and am—one with two parallel ways of being. I was always good at math and have always been able to connect with what many call the "left side" of my brain. I demonstrate analytical traits, particularly when they're warranted. I am a planner. I like to assess information or responsibilities, organize the information/tasks, develop a plan, and execute. And I have typically been praised for the ability to manage and maximize resources, without question.

However, I am equally connected to what many call the "right side" of my brain. I am creative at heart! I love color. I love fashion. I love music! As you can imagine, when I stepped into the world of business, particularly as a woman, those traits were not readily embraced. It was assumed that creativity was associated with exceptional emotional displays and a temperamental disposition. It was assumed that as a creative, I would lack focus. And with my love of color and fashion that I would lack intellectual substance. I will never forget when a powerful community stakeholder described my personhood as an interesting marketing approach that was *attention seeking*. As a part of our special events, I have been asked to perform on occasion. I can't count the number of times corporate-minded

---

3    Bart de Langhe and Philip Fernbach, "The Dangers of Categorical Thinking," *Harvard Business Review*, September 2019, accessed May 17, 2023, https://hbr.org/2019/09/the-dangers-of-categorical-thinking.

individuals have attended and looked at me in disbelief and dismay on the stage. But rather than say my unique approach wasn't palatable for *them*, instead, they would say I needed to abandon that side of myself and defer to my direct reports, whose communication styles and ways of being were more resonant with their personal preferences.

Here's what I resolved: I could work anywhere if I was going to conform to coloring inside the imposed lines. There was no need to be a social entrepreneur and start a new nonprofit if I was going to color inside the lines. Instead, I embraced the opportunity to color outside the lines. Why can't a woman be creative, while leading effectively? Why couldn't a woman appreciate the interior design of her office *and* enjoy reviewing spreadsheets? How come a woman can't interpret financial statements *and* write the music jingles for her company?

So over the past twenty-five years, starting my own nonprofit afforded me the ability to color outside the lines. I could lead my nonprofit, oversee the entirety of its operations but also bring another aspect of myself to help the organization fulfill its mission. I am a musician. I am a singer. I am a performer. I am a songwriter. Twenty years into the nonprofit, I finally found a way to leverage those strengths. First, I integrated the performing arts into our youth development programs, creating a more holistic experience for children that embraces diversity in abilities and intelligence types. I became the songwriter, coproducer, and recording voice for all of our nonprofit's promotional campaigns. I became the executive producer of our agency's promotional videos.

I gave myself *permission* to incorporate all of me into all I do.

Lines continued to be imposed. Questions were raised about my roles in the artistic sides of the organization. I was labeled "attention seeking," "unfocused," and unable to share the spotlight with others who contributed far less. I was initially baffled. Usually, the chief executive's role in the organization is to be an external presence, and in many cases, to be the face of the organization. So I realized the issue was not with my presence. It was with what my presence represented. I colored outside the lines.

And I continued to color outside the lines. I continued to stand on our brand. I decided it was more prudent to make a splash into what was already an oversaturated market, rather than be a duplication of a picture that had already been created. And since 2020, our campaigns have reached 100 million people!

## QUESTIONS FOR REFLECTION

1.  In what areas of your personal and professional lives do you feel the lines being drawn for you?

2.  In which of those areas would you like to "color outside the lines"?

3.  In which of those areas do you see the capacity to color outside the lines?

4.  In what areas are you already coloring outside the lines?

5.  In what areas could you color outside the lines but are not yet doing so? What is holding you back? What opportunities are you missing as a result of holding back?

## CLOSING

Remember—in order to truly define and stand on your brand, your brand should be authentic. In order to be authentic, it is important to bring your whole self to the work. Your call is unique to you because it embodies your unique traits in action. Today, we give ourselves *permission* to acknowledge and embrace our personal canvases or pictures. When we accept and embrace that the picture is ours to color and the finished product represents our call, then we move forward with the freedom and confidence to color outside the lines, be unique, and stand by the vision and the product.

> **When we embrace that the picture is ours to color and represents our call, we move forward with freedom and confidence to color outside the lines.**

## Own Your Authority

As I cultivated those creative sides of my brand, I also wrestled with the imposed lines of staying in that lane. There were some who only wanted to see that side of the brand. In other words, "Be the 'pretty face' of the organization but do not lead this organization." "Use your nurturing personality to connect with children and families, and even to nurture your supporting team. But do not hold them accountable. Do not expect productivity. Just be inspirational."

However, I come from a culture that can be paternalistic and overemphasize the importance of respect for elders. When I would require accountability, I was often met with a huff or dismissed as if I hadn't lived enough years to bring insight to the conversation, or to lead. I battled with these distortions even when I had more practical experience and training in the area of discussion than the others. I was told directly and indirectly, "Let the men of the organization and the elders direct the operations."

Women leaders are challenged from every angle. We are challenged by our superiors and our direct reports. Some days it seems like everybody is attempting to strip away any sense of confidence or competence we have. We walk in the space of double standards. Others impose perfection on us, while whatever others contribute is accepted, acknowledged, and praised. Oftentimes, the tactic is designed to wear us down and force us to walk around constantly apologizing for the leadership positions we have earned. Many times, the intent is to manipulate us into holding a title in name only.

It is tempting to bend to the pressure or even become more reactive and bitter. Sometimes it is tempting to walk around oblivious, as though you don't see it or hear it. Be kind to those who report to you but also be vigilant. Be aware of overt disrespect and hostility. But also, be aware of the more subtle manipulations people will use in the hope you will cede your true authority or apologize for it.

Pay particular attention to your interactions with your direct reports. Whereas we endeavor to create an organizational culture where everyone feels valued and excited about their job, do not forget that *you* are the one tasked with the responsibility to lead. Consequences for decisions made will fall on *you* first. If a decision is mishandled, some of the questions you will be asked by your superiors are 1) should you have known better? and 2) were you acting with the level of competence and judgment expected for *your* position? What your direct reports said and thought will not shield you from potential negative or dire consequences.

Here are a few wisdoms I've learned along the way on how to own my authority.

1.  Be able to discern whether your direct reports are asking questions to seek clarification, control the conversation, or to build a case to form an evaluation of you. Oftentimes

this tactic is employed to pressure you into second-guessing every decision you make. This can undermine your credibility and give people what they believe to be the justification not to listen to what you have to say. Speak to the items relevant to that person's job description and how that description advances the mission and vision of the organization. If you are operating ethically and responsibly, you do not owe them an explanation of your job performance/personality/vision/strategy.

2. Be able to discern whether your direct reports need more attention and/or resources, or if they are attempting to manipulate you through the tactic of excessive neediness. This tactic is often used to manipulate you into helping people do their work for them or with them. They often employ this tactic because they cannot stand the fact that you have the authority to delegate tasks to them. Empower them to be self-motivated and directed. Hold them accountable for doing their work, doing it independently, and exercising the appropriate level of professional judgment for the position.

3. Resist the temptation to want to be liked and accepted. That is often the desire that drives us to overexplain ourselves instead of making the tough calls. Instead, strive to be fair. Surround yourself with people who can guide you on the right time to talk and the right time to act. Add a great attorney and HR professional to your circle so you can be fair, ethical, and serious about your business! You are very busy!

## QUESTIONS FOR REFLECTION

1.  How do you currently respond to direct reports when they ask questions about your decisions or decision-making processes? What aspects of your response process do you believe need to be increased? Which aspects do you believe need to be refined?

2.  How well do your direct reports understand your brand and the brand of the organization?

3.  Do you see your brand as a way to define and communicate your approach to leading?

4.  How can you, or do you, use your brand to define and communicate your leadership approach?

5.  What sorts of verbal and nonverbal approaches can you use to stand by your brand when you are communicating with your direct reports?

## CLOSING

Being challenged will be a recurring theme throughout this book. It is a part of leading. It is particularly a part of leading as a woman. Though the reactions may be fierce and negative initially, they do tend to subside—if you stand confidently and boldly by your brand. Sometimes the silence is coupled with isolation, but that is okay. As Nicholas Klein once said, "First they ignore you. Then they ridicule you. Then they attack you. Then you win!" But remember this—when you stand by your brand, and you give yourself *permission* to own your authority as a leader, you position yourself to attract the type of people who are comfortable with your brand. And people learn to trust in your competence.

# Branding Your Call and Preserving the Standard

In order to build a brand with lasting power and lead in a compelling manner, standards cannot be avoided. It is important for others to know who you are. That is why we define ourselves as a part of building our brand. That is the building block for defining and branding the call. People need to understand your call—what it is, and what it means to you, if they are going to support you in fulfilling your call.

In the last chapter, we discussed defining what you want for your life. Once you know what you want, it must be communicated, and communicated unapologetically. In coloring outside the lines, you demonstrate how your brand and your call are different. You demonstrate why the call has value and why others should support your call—through service, patronage, or otherwise.

A part of defining your call must include setting a standard. You must set boundaries of what is acceptable and what is not acceptable. What level of service or product value is acceptable and what is not. What level of communication is acceptable and what is not. Your standards are the key to establishing competence, consistency, and confidence in your brand.

And just as women are challenged as authority figures, our standards are also challenged. Like others will use excessive questioning, neediness, and other forms of resistance to challenge authority, they engage in the same behaviors around standards. The introduction of quality standards is often met with "Why?" or

"That's impossible," or "They don't need all that," or "They wouldn't appreciate it anyway."

As a CEO in the nonprofit space, I am met with such resistance almost daily. There are many who believe one's income determines whether or not they are deserving of dignity, respect, and high-quality programs. As a woman CEO, I work with people who feel empowered to bend and break the policies I set. They may dismiss my policies, considering them as undeserving of the same level of adherence to standards because they come from a woman. Sometimes the complaints and resistance can be so persistent there are days we ask ourselves, "Why even bother?"

But do not allow complaining customers or complaining employees to lure you into the illusion of "damned if you do, and damned if you don't." Always remain focused on your product and your brand. Without consideration to the complaining or disappointing behavior or substandard performance of others, ask yourself at decision time: Does this represent excellence? Does this product show the best representation of me, my brand, or the organization I'm leading?

If it does not, then continue to work in a way that represents excellence—even when you are not in complete control of the decision making or the result. Regardless of what you see others do, go the extra mile. Hold others accountable, even when they resist. Remember—people who continuously challenge the standard are banking on wearing you down so you fall to the level of mediocrity that makes *them* feel comfortable.

On the most frustrating days, keep pushing! Be guided by principle and not the whims of people—particularly people who have already shown you they care nothing about the mission you're trying to accomplish. Sometimes we're afraid our standards will alienate or drive away people who we feel we need at the time. But compromising will not help you to hang on to them. Actually, people who consistently reject your brand and your standards are hanging on to *you* until they feel they no longer need to. Remember—low expectations and the rejection of excellence uplifts no one.

## QUESTIONS FOR REFLECTION

1.  Do your supporting staff or people in your immediate support circle know what your call is? If they do not, why don't they? What is holding them back from knowing what your call is?

2.  What are your standards for your personal brand and professional brand? What are your quality standards within the area you lead? Do the people in your personal and professional circles know your quality standards? Why or why not?

3.  How do you respond when your standards are questioned or not followed? What strategies do you use to uphold your standards? What strategies do you need to develop?

## CLOSING

Every time you divert from your brand and standards, you divert from your call. It is extremely difficult to make progress when we continue to veer off the path. There are many fads/organizations/products/people that come and go, which erodes trust in new ideas, leaders, and leadership approaches. Remember, in order to develop trust and move forward in your call, you must remain consistent. Show a consistent commitment to your call. Give yourself *permission* to define and enforce your standards. Enforce them consistently, and again, you will attract people who ascribe to those standards and are willing to help you move closer to fulfilling your call.

# Sow Responsibly

Building your brand and standing by your brand is hard work. Committing to fulfilling your unique call is time consuming. Building a brand to advance your call requires laser-focused commitment. Your time must be used strategically, or you run the risk of being defined in relation to the call/brand of others.

> **We feel obligated to help as we have been helped and to help because we have been hurt.**

Giving must be balanced and intentional. But many times, as women leaders, it is difficult to discern when and how much to give back. We think of all the people who helped us along our personal/professional journeys, as well as the people who have hurt us. We feel obligated to help as we have been helped and to help because we have been hurt. We wrestle with when to say yes, and how to say no. As a social entrepreneur, the struggle can be even more challenging. What do you do when giving is a part of your brand and your call?

One principle that has helped me strike balance is refusing to sow into people who are only concerned with sowing into themselves. People who only intend to sow into themselves exhibit behaviors that women should watch carefully. Sometimes they cannot say thank you or refuse to acknowledge the contributions of others. In that case, it is reasonable to surmise such a person would not recognize the most precious gems you have to share. Another sign to look out for is people who dominate the conversation with getting their needs met and leave little room for dialogue, alternative perspectives, or alternative choices. Also be cognizant of those who only prioritize their time and needs and continuously create inconvenience for those who are seeking to help them, without concern or consideration. Many of those people refuse to make any accommodations if it means inconvenience for them.

Women—you are not obligated to help people advance their personal goals, when they are oblivious to the lives, feelings, and concerns of those who surround them. Often, you will notice that people who expect support but give none enter helping relationships with unreasonable expectations in the first place. These are often the type of people who, no matter how you help, it will never be enough. They often focus on what you did not do, or cannot do for them, rather than what you have done. They will often expect you to do all the lifting and refuse to take sufficient responsibility for their role in their own success. If you are not careful, they will take everything you have and drain you to the point where you lose energy, as well as sight of other people, projects, and passions that also require your attention. You will find yourself diverting from your call, not to serve but to be used.

## QUESTIONS FOR REFLECTION

1. In your list of standards (or branding), did you include your terms for helping others? If you did not, why not?

2. Why do you think including your terms for helping others might be critical to establishing your brand and standards?

3. How much time do you give back to helping others fulfill their calls?

4. Do you have a process for how you accept requests to give back to another person or organization?

5. Do you have requirements for the person/organization you are helping? How clear are you in communicating those expectations? If you are not clear, why not?

6. In what areas do you need to more clearly and confidently communicate and enforce your standards for giving back?

7. If you develop those areas, how much extra time will you have each week for fulfilling your call?

## CLOSING

When you define your brand and standards, and stand by them, then you find yourself less vulnerable to those who want to use you as a tool to fulfill their self-serving desires. But these standards cannot be kept in your head. You must clearly explain them before the relationship begins. And it helps to be consistent in how you engage in helping/supporting other people. Remember—how you say *yes* and *no* are a part of your brand. How you say *yes* and *no* communicates your true standards. Remember—time is a precious resource that cannot be recovered. Give yourself *permission* to guard your time and sow carefully!

# Balance Your Transactions

When you are serious about your brand and are intentionally building that brand to help you advance the call you have accepted in your life, you naturally expect the people who you consistently support to at least verbally support your brand. If you're selling a product, it is natural to expect those whom you have patronized should patronize you as well. You certainly would expect those whom you patronized would be proud to acknowledge you as one of their customers.

That, however, hasn't always been my experience. I remember working with a vendor who was a well-known recording artist. He listened to some of the music I wrote and recorded during a live performance. After listening, he offered to produce the songs. He knew my goal at the time was to shop this music out to radio stations and to record labels as well.

He provided me with the product, and I paid for it. But he told me not to let anyone know it was his product. That struck me as extremely odd. However, working in the music business, you'll find that a lot of things will strike you as odd. I found out later the product had some issues. Along the way, I became connected with other well-connected individuals in the music business, who still advocate for me and support me to this day. The producer told my representative and advocate that he invested little in the product because he didn't think I, or my music, was headed anywhere. Meanwhile, I observed how he uplifted and used his presence in the business to propel so many others who did not bring the amount of talent I brought to the table. Most were singers only. I could sing, arrange, write, and perform. My intent is not to reduce their talent but to only say, based on the most conservative estimate, I was equally deserving. It was angering and very hurtful.

Yes, process the emotions but do not remain frustrated when you invest your time, support, energy, credibility, and money into businesses, entrepreneurs, and leaders who do not reciprocate. I very well understand how painful it is when you acknowledge people, particularly in a public space or on a public platform, and they do not acknowledge you back. Sometimes it seems like they're making a point to exclude you by acknowledging everyone *except* you.

You cannot control what other people do, nor will you always understand why people do the things they do. So, instead, try the following:

1. Replace the time and energy you are investing in building other people's visibility and brands with investing in your *own* brand/business. Be the type of business/brand that people gravitate to. Understand, if you are using your patronage to leverage someone else's brand, they will see right through you.

2. Spend wisely. Invest your money in people and businesses that invest in *you*. If you are good enough to provide financial support to their business, you are good enough to be acknowledged as a customer and congratulated for your milestones. If there is a disconnect here, then have an honest conversation. Because there may be times where your brands do, in fact, conflict. Your brand could hurt theirs, and their brand could hurt yours. Weigh the pros and cons and continue to look for vendors whose brands and values align with yours. In the long run, you'll go much further in advancing your vision.

3. Focus less on what others are saying/not saying and doing/not doing. Many times, people are talking positively about your brand/business out of your presence. Sometimes because of their own insecurities, they don't want *you* to know about it.

4. Be an example yourself. When you send out invitations to your business page, or support your business in any way, be sure to extend support and acknowledgment to those whom you ask for support. Thoughtfulness is the key to cultivating and keeping good customers/supporters.

## QUESTIONS FOR REFLECTION

1. Do you know who the most loyal supporters of your brand, standards, and call are? How do you define support?

2. Do you see any commonalities between your supporters? Do you see any commonalities in the aspects of your brand, standards, and call that they choose to support?

3. What types of support do they provide to further your brand, standards, and call?

4. How do you show your supporters that you appreciate them? Do you have an intentional method of making sure you show appreciation regularly? What could that look like?

5. Are there any people in your circle who are not supporting your brand, standards, and call as they should? Are you making efforts to support their brands, standards, and their calls? How can you scale back that support and reinvest time in promoting your own brand, standards, and call?

## CLOSING

How you spend your time and energy are very important. How you spend your money and promote your brand are also very important. Every time you endorse someone who doesn't endorse you or your brand, you disincentivize others to support your brand. Time diverted from building supporters of your brand and standards is time diverted from fulfilling your call. Give yourself *permission* to say no to those who say no to you. We are very busy! We have no time to waste in fulfilling our calls. Give yourself *permission* to invest wisely and invest in *you*!

> **When you endorse someone who doesn't endorse you, you disincentivize others to support your brand. Time diverted from building supporters is time diverted from fulfilling your call.**

# Getting the Most out of Your Brand: Priorities, Productivity, and Price

As we discussed, time is a very precious resource that cannot be replaced. Placing a laser focus on building our brands, establishing standards, and fulfilling our calls requires tough choices. We talked about how we can say no to external people demanding or taking advantage of our time and resources. But we also must take a long, hard look at our abilities to juggle and manage our personal responsibilities. How do we fit it all in?

One way we can free up time to build and establish our brands (and ultimately our calls) is by resisting the temptation to *do it all!* Many societal voices shame women for not fulfilling every gendered role, plus some more. In answering our calls, we must grant ourselves *permission* to set priorities. We need to ask ourselves, "Is this function essential to me? Is this function essential to the functioning of my household? Does this priority meet an essential necessity? Is this function essential to me answering my call? Or has this priority been suggested to me or imposed on me by someone who cannot impact my well being or household, meet an essential necessity, or further me in answering my call?" We must give ourselves *permission* to decide what we are able to do, what we need to do, and what can be delegated.

Oftentimes we procrastinate in delegation because initially, it takes a bit of time. Often, in the workplace and otherwise, people are assigned to positions or roles that do not draw out their strengths. Sometimes we are frustrated by coworkers, team members, and those who report to us because they are underperforming in the areas where we expected them to shine. It takes time to process the strengths of those around us and then figure out the best way to utilize those strengths. So we take the easy route (at least initially) and say, "I'll do it myself."

Instead, view it as an opportunity to show your ingenuity. It is not always possible, but in many cases, there are opportunities to find out what our direct reports or other supporting persons do well and leverage those strengths. We may not gain all of what we need or expect, but finding out what they do well and building off that does indeed take something off our plate. That is something to celebrate and notate.

Another challenge that gets in the way of us delegating is price. Sometimes we are hesitant to pay for services that, from a societal standpoint, should be carried out by the individual. Sometimes we scrutinize price but do not consider the cost of lowered productivity. We need to ask ourselves: How much faster could I promote or increase my rate of pay if I were to delegate and pay for household maintenance services? How much more time would I have to focus my time, energy, and attention on answering and fulfilling my call? How much more time would I have to process my emotions and connect more with the members of my household? How much less money would I spend on "self-medication" (in whatever form) because I would be less stressed to begin with?

When we revisit our definitions of ourselves, our wants, our brand, and our standards, we remember we cannot be everything to everyone. We are more likely to find satisfaction when we find those areas in our lives where we function best and refine/pursue those. We are also more likely to sustain that satisfaction when we engage those in our circles intentionally, delegating and leveraging what they also do best. When we find intentional ways to focus on what brings out the best in ourselves and others, then we stand on our brand, communicate our brand and standards more effectively, and are better able to galvanize others to help us fulfill our calls.

## QUESTIONS FOR REFLECTION

1. What tasks are you assuming in both your professional and personal lives that you should not be doing in the first place? Why are you doing those tasks? Why haven't they been delegated?

2. What tasks are you holding on to that could be delegated? Why are you holding on to them?

3. What disposable income could be reallocated to support you in tasks that are not advancing your brand, standards, or call?

4. What individuals are in your personal and/or professional circles with talents you are underutilizing? How can you start leveraging those strengths?

# Key Points to Remember

Throughout this chapter, I've talked about how so many voices and pressures seek to dilute our brands and deafen our calls! They attempt to intimidate us, preventing us from establishing and enforcing the standards that position us to fulfill our calls. Notions of what it means to be a woman, a woman leader, a woman boss, etc. make it so hard to move forward in peace, and with joy. Ladies, no matter your personal style, your way of being, your goals, or your approach to leading, know that you do not have to follow the template. *You* are the template!

- Because you're "not for everybody" anyway, go ahead and color outside the lines!

- Own your authority. You are in a position of authority because you are capable, and you are enough.

- Preserve and protect your standards. Without standards, there is no consistent message or way of being. Without consistency, there is no brand.

- Time is a precious resource. Give back to others but pick your activities by intentionally aligning them with your brand, your standards, and your call.

- Know when to delegate so you can devote sufficient time to your brand.

- Balance your transactions. Continue to invest in *you*!

\*\*\*

I would like to share a poem I wrote a few years ago, which I have reworked and titled "I Stand by My Brand!" The hope is you will develop the language necessary to stand by *your* brand.

# I Stand by My Brand

*Eyes that pierce through the surface of dishonesty and game,*

*they're mine. They're a part of my brand. I stand by my brand!*

*A heart that loves but does not play;*

*it's mine. It's a part of my brand. I stand by my brand!*

*A will that, for some, is too strong;*

*it's mine. It's a part of my brand. I stand by my brand!*

*A point of view that, for some, cuts too deep;*

*it's mine. It's a part of my brand. I stand by my brand!*

*I won't apologize for embracing myself as I am, for*

*rejecting anyone's imposed standards.*

*I won't apologize for being comfortable with my unique combination of femininity,*

*authentic, bold, with unbridled intensity.*

*I will continue to embrace candid "in-your-face" sass*

*that in the next moment can be masked*

*to protect the heart and psyche,*

*all while "surviving"*

*in a world that, today, is too small to handle the full expression of the bold, beautiful, woman.*

*A world that fears our boldness,*

*failing to recognize the same "fiery" passion that burns also warms, drawing others in, restoring them to wholeness.*

*But until then, my skin, my nose, my heart, my will, my point of view, and my fiery sass is mine. It's a part of my brand. I stand by my brand!*

*And every day, I will live in reverence of every ancestor subject to overt and covert oppression, often in the face of scorn and ridicule,*

*so I would have the opportunity to say, "It's a part of my brand. I stand by my brand!"*

\*\*\*

# Elevation in Action

As we close out this chapter, I have some challenges that will help you exercise permission in standing by your brand, establishing and enforcing your standards, and moving closer to fulfilling your call.

1. Develop a script of how you will respond the next time someone questions your personal brand or the brand of your organization. Try to keep your language positive while reinforcing your brand and your commitment to your brand.

2. Develop a list of ways you can incorporate more of your personality into your professional brand. Describe areas where you can "push the envelope" to distinguish yourself from others doing similar work.

3. Develop a strategy for how you will enforce your quality standards. How will you communicate them to others? What will you do when they are violated? How will you process out the situation after the violation has been addressed?

4. Develop a process for how you will engage with those asking for assistance or mentorship. How will you interview them? What are your factors for determining if you will move forward in the relationship? What are your expectations for the relationship? What is the time limit? How will you terminate helping relationships?

5. Develop a process for how you will patronize the services of other vendors. What are your reciprocation expectations?

6. Name one activity you can delegate to make more time to advance your brand and call.

CHAPTER 3

# *PEACE WHILE SWIMMING WITH SHARKS*

One critical strategy in preserving my brand and carrying out my call was the ability to bring mental focus to the work I do. I learned very early in my professional career I could not bring the necessary level of focus without peace. Peace is not something that comes automatically. We live with a number of distractions. Some distractions are random. Others are designed to divert our focus and derail us from carrying out the calls we are uniquely created and destined to fulfill.

Some situations are just distractions, but we also encounter sharks. Sharks circle around looking to devour and destroy. In our professional circles, it's no different. Sharks intend to kill our spirits, kill our ideas, kill our contributions, and kill our dreams. Swimming with the sharks around us can cause us to become so focused on protecting ourselves that we do not seize opportunities to grow, contribute, and rise. We can become so bitter that we have little chance of attracting the people who will help us answer and fulfill the calls on our lives.

In this chapter, I will talk about various ways I have been able to keep my own peace intact while swimming with sharks. I will talk about how I limited the access of sharks into my personal and professional spaces. Part of our success will depend on being able to discern when to avoid sharks, when to swim with them, and when to attack back.

# Access Denied: Keeping the Sharks out of Your Inner Circle

To avoid sharks, we must choose wisely those who we allow to occupy our space and our time. Vibes, ways of being, feelings, and points of view can be infectious. We have to identify those individuals who leave us feeling inspired and those who leave us feeling drained. We must discern those who challenge us to be better, from those who critique to hurt and discourage.

As women, we are often pressured into inviting sharks into our personal space, our families, our business, and our bedrooms. We are told (directly and indirectly) to be overly accommodating, overly forgiving, because that is what nice, caring women do. We wrestle with the questions "Am I being too callous?" "What will this person do if I am not in their life?" "What will this person do without this position?" We are judged for holding individuals accountable in our organizations. And sometimes we are pressured to affiliate with those who may offer an external benefit to our circles, even when their presence creates internal damage.

Keeping the sharks out of your inner circle is a daily journey. Even when relationships seem to be working well, learn the habit of saying the relationship is working well, "right now." Relationships evolve, and sometimes relationships corrode. Though misconceptions, misunderstandings, and reconciliations do occur, do not fail to ask the question, *Is this person a shark?* Can this person do the damage of a shark, intentionally or otherwise?

Denying sharks access to my inner circle has been one of the keys to securing my physical, mental, emotional, and spiritual freedom. Over fifteen years ago, my mom and I were riding into work, and I filled her in on an ongoing relationship conflict that continued to escalate and become more complicated and entangled. She listened while I ranted.

Then, when I was finally done, she gently said, "Don't waste all your young years focusing on the foolishness of people who ten, twenty, and thirty years from now, will still be engaged in nothing but foolishness. Forget them and enjoy your life."

My mom's short statement challenged me to ask the hard questions.

1. Why do I care?

2. Why should I care?

3. Why is this worth my time?

Sometimes, as women, we hold on to entangled emotions because once we disengage mentally and emotionally, then we disengage physically and move on. Today, give yourself *permission* to be okay with cutting off the sharks in a world where women are often expected to put relationships (even toxic relationships) above their well-being, and their ambitions.

Give yourself permission to be okay with cutting off sharks!

Giving yourself *permission* to say and believe, "This is not worth my time or engagement." This belief unlocks the key to our emotional wellness, and our peace. Why? Because then we begin to, unapologetically, only make space in our minds and hearts for people who bring support, empathy, and wisdom into our lives. We only entertain the opinions of those who would value, love, and support us when we have nothing to offer them in return.

Such permission frees us from the emotional rollercoaster of dealing with fake friends, superficial spectators, liars, opportunists, and haters for the "hell of it." It frees us to attract people who do not need and are not looking for anything in return. It frees us to attract people who make themselves accessible to talk, listen, share, advocate, and intervene in an immediate time of need. We build relationships rather than rack up affiliations and associations that would not stand the test of time or challenges.

When we free ourselves from investing in time on roads to nowhere, we become more serious about our goals. When I did this, I decided to go back to school and also began working more seriously on the business that I love, writing music that I love, and embarking on countless other adventures that continue to evolve. Cutting the sharks out of our circles requires us to take a hard look at our lives, where we've been, where we are headed, and what regret might come of it. But it's worth it because we find ourselves in the right mental space to learn, grow, create, and continue to strive for better.

## QUESTIONS FOR REFLECTION

1. What sharks are in your "circle"? By *circle*, we mean close proximity, having access to information or space that can seriously impact your life.

2. Why are these sharks in your circle?

3. What have you done to eliminate these sharks from your circle?

4. If you have not eliminated such sharks, what is holding you back?

5. If the sharks are in a position where you do not have the authority to eliminate them altogether, how can you restrict their access to information and other factors that negatively impact you or progress toward your call?

## CLOSING

When we think about chapter 1 and the process of self-understanding, that process puts us on the path to discern what is good for us and what is not. Now that we've explored who we are, what we want, and where we want to go, surrounding ourselves with the right people is imperative. We must carefully position ourselves and protect ourselves from any threats to advancing our individual missions and carrying out our calls. Let this thought give you the *permission* you need to protect yourself from the sharks. Your feelings, your contributions, your dreams and your call are all *worth it*!

# Permission to *Stay Home*

Another pressure women contend with is putting themselves in the way of negative, nasty people for the sake of the family or the community. For example, holiday tables are often a space where family members are forced together, whether or not they like each other or have anything in common. Too often, the differences in lifestyle, worldview, and experiences take center stage at holiday events. Tension often lies under the surface or escalates to passive-aggressive sniping or even direct confrontation.

But these events are not limited to some family events. As women, we can find ourselves in similar situations when we participate in community activities—oftentimes community activities that were said to help build relationships and propel professional goals. In these instances, I would find myself as the "new person" in rooms, sitting alone. People would walk past me as if I wasn't even there. Or I would find myself being "hypervisible"—being asked probing, prodding, and even rude questions. Snide remarks were made about my hair, my clothes, the size and scale of my organization, and my dating status.

And while we are under verbal and nonverbal assault, we are often forced to witness how so many others benefit from participation in the very same social groups and organizations. We see their businesses and brands promoted. We see their businesses booked for future events. In my situation, I would mention to some of the group members one on one why I was being overlooked. At that point, I would get awkward giggles.

Give yourself *permission* to ask, "Why am I even here? Why am I putting myself through this?" Give yourself *permission* to say, "I'm staying home."

Today, let us give ourselves *permission* to decline *any* situation where:

1. We are insulted directly or through innuendos and nonverbal attacks.

2. We feel any sense of coercion or threat—direct or implied.

3. We feel like we must watch our back or our possessions.

4. We feel like we have to defend ourselves or explain our point of view or lifestyle.

5. We only feel valued if we are doing something or giving something. We don't feel comfortable to "just be."

6. We feel tension in the air—whether it's directed toward us or not.

7. Antagonists are allowed to freely antagonize with no accountability.

8. One person or group controls all the terms for engagement and participation.

9. We are required to bend and adapt, overlook, or make excuses/allowance for poor behavior.

10. We are consistently required to carry more than our share of the load.

11. We have to act out of character to get along or survive.

12. Our contributions are ignored or hidden.

13. We are vilified, ignored, or ostracized for speaking "truth to power."

## QUESTIONS FOR REFLECTION

1. Did any of the circumstances listed above resonate with you? Which? Why?

2. In what spaces did the circumstances listed above apply to you? Why do you or did you tolerate such behavior?

3. In what ways can you give yourself *permission* to "stay home"? If it is a place you must go, such as your place of employment, how can you avoid the sharks anyway?

## CLOSING

We cannot live our best life carrying the baggage of negative energy. We cannot make progress in our personal or professional lives, as long as we seek out the very sharks that disrupt our peace. In order to attain and enjoy answering our call and carrying it out, we have to let go of faulty assumptions that have only created a false appearance of unity. We need to have honest conversations about abuse in all its forms. We need not feel guilty about knowing better and doing better. No sense of obligation should motivate us to enter an environment that we *know* is neither productive nor edifying. Give yourself *permission* to let those sharks go so you can heal, build, and win!

> We cannot make progress in our personal or professional lives, as long as we seek out the very sharks that disrupt our peace.

# Seeing and Acknowledging the Signs

In leadership, it is imperative that we can see a shark before it gets too close. I often hear from people who are bewildered and blindsided by betrayals and blowups they never saw coming. Though some betrayals and blowups cannot be avoided, here are a few of the wisdoms we can use to avoid the sharks altogether or prepare for any potential confrontations.

1. Be wary of people who constantly interrupt you while you're speaking, consistently pretend they don't hear what you have to say, or consistently pretend not to notice your accomplishments. Be especially wary when they do not treat others the same way.

2. Be wary of people who spend more time highlighting what they believe to be your shortcomings than your contributions. Also be wary of people who exaggerate what they believe to be your faults, particularly in comparison to how they perceive and relate to others.

If a person cannot stand the sound of your voice, the content of your statements, your presence, or they can't stand to see what you do, then guess what? They can't stand you, what you stand for, or the fact that *you* have been gifted with presence, power, and authority.

The tactics above are designed to do some or all of the following:

1. To tell you, "I don't like you."

2. To tell you, "I don't value what you value."

3. To tell you, "I only value it if you are not involved."

Or, to:

4. Slowly dismantle your power or authority by whittling away at your confidence.

Often as women we are frustrated about why we have not accomplished more or why our dreams haven't been actualized. Sometimes we are delayed in fulfilling our calls because we spend too much time trying to convince the wrong people to be part of the team. We spend too much time trying to convince the wrong people to value what we value.

Remember—if they are not *for* us, they are *against* us. Every minute wasted with people who don't care for us, our values, or our visions is a minute taken from spending time and growing with those who *do*!

## QUESTIONS FOR REFLECTION

1. When you enter a physical or virtual space, how do you read the temperature in the room?

2. Do you assess your allies as well as the "sharks" in the room? What signs alert you to the sharks that are ready to directly attack you and your call?

3. What sharks are circling you? Are they mostly in your personal life or professional life? If they are sharks in your personal life, how are they impacting your professional life or your ability to answer your call?

4. How do you respond to sharks when they show signs of attack mode? How do you avoid them or prepare for confrontation?

## CLOSING

When the signs show us we are dealing with a shark, we need not second-guess what we see and hear. We must give ourselves *permission* to protect ourselves by establishing sufficient distance. We must give ourselves *permission* to disengage and move on with our dreams and our lives. When we must coexist with people who show they are not *for* us, we can still move on in our hearts. We can intentionally surround ourselves with people who do value us and our calls. One essential protective strategy we can use when we can't avoid a shark altogether is to restrict the information they receive. We can protect ourselves best when we give ourselves *permission* to believe our bodies, minds, spirits, and calls are worth protecting; we are not hateful beings for calling a shark a *shark*.

# Recognizing Sharks in Disguise

As a social entrepreneur, I am constantly tasked with balancing the interest of the organization with the interests of the community, and our clients/residents. This requires me to view a situation through multiple lenses simultaneously. Long story short, I've been in a lot of situations where people were not always transparent about their interests. Frankly, I've witnessed a lot of situations where people pretended to represent vulnerable people, when they were really only using those vulnerable people for their own gain. Sometimes the gain was financial. Other times the gain was notoriety or attention. And still other times, the gain was fulfilling a need to be needed. Some strategies we can use to discern include understanding that the loudest voice is not always the most passionate soul. Women, we serve ourselves well when we know the difference between advocacy and misplaced rage, self-promotion, or jockeying for self-gain.

Recognizing sharks in disguise will be essential to the survival of our peace, and likely our calls. Openness to the wrong external players can undermine our progress or destroy our organizations altogether. And, when we think about the capacity for harm that can be inflicted, we know sharks in disguise can evoke strong emotions in us. As infuriating as it can be to sit and listen to people who we know are not involved for the right reasons, it is tempting to take on a certain "edge" when we're being assaulted from every direction.

## QUESTIONS FOR REFLECTION

1. In your professional space, are sharks in disguise lauded and celebrated? If so, how does it make you feel? How does it make you feel about fulfilling your call within the workspace?

2. How do you respond to sharks in disguise in your professional work or in your service to the community? Have your responses made any difference in how those sharks are regarded or handled in such spaces?

3. What adjustments do you think you could make in dealing with sharks in disguise to further the fulfillment of your own call?

4. How confident do you feel about dealing with sharks in disguise? What steps could you take to increase that confidence?

## CLOSING

When faced with a shark in disguise, let us resist the temptation to fight for the last word, or try to get in the last dig. Let us resist the temptation to assemble and feed an army of defenders. Some "sympathizers" are also sharks in disguise who only want to get close enough to discover and exploit our vulnerabilities later when they feel the time is right. Or those types of disguised sharks will distance themselves in our time of need, when they've collected all the data on our lives that they feel they can use for their own purposes.

Instead, let us seize the opportunity to show a counternarrative. We can demonstrate how to translate passion into action. We can demonstrate the difference between being aggressive and taking authority. We give ourselves *permission* to see a shark for who he or she is, but we should also keep our eyes on the bigger picture. Remember it takes no talent to tear down, but it does take tremendous effort, talent, and insight to build. Let us continue to build on the move!

# Managing Shark Attacks

Sharks have a myriad of ways to attack us and our progress toward fulfilling our calls. Sometimes they heckle us and our efforts. Other times they come with completely off-base assertions, which are designed to provoke us to fly off the handle. And when confrontation occurs, they will attempt to tear down our reputations by playing the victim to every person who will listen. In this series of thoughts, it is imperative we give ourselves *permission* to be. We can address attacks, but we must do so with intentionality. In this section, we will discuss two types of sharks: the heckling shark and the manipulating shark.

Heckling sharks question, mock, or devalue our accomplishments, expertise, contributions, credentials, or business. They like to give backhanded compliments or tell us how we could've answered/fulfilled our call much better, but they never present any new ideas/products/services or a call of their own. They like to complain about the working conditions but never offer any solutions. Oftentimes, their heckling reflects their resentment of us for, having the audacity to acknowledge, accept, and fulfill our calls. Our audacity shames them as they are often paralyzed by fear, lack of motivation, or incompetence.

As frustrating as these hecklers can be, let us resist the temptation to be consumed with their hate. Instead, we can invite them out of their spectator chairs to do the hard work. We can invite them to show everyone how it's done. We can make it a point to ask them about how their projects are going and about the contributions they are or should be making.

This thought is inspired by one of my most revered mentors, Faris Alami. I called him up, frustrated at individuals who continued to denigrate both me and my family for founding Center of Hope and remaining active in the organization's development and growth. That particular day, Faris told me, "The people who question your journey are most often the ones who are insecure about their own journeys." Faris opened my eyes, and then I gave myself *permission* to be comfortable in my own journey. That permission led to me dismissing the notions of those heckling sharks, so I could enjoy fulfilling the call in front of me.

When dealing with manipulating sharks, it is essential we give ourselves *permission* not to provide an explanation for every person who wants to invent a problem. Part of that permission includes resisting the urge to atone for every manipulative shark who claims we "did them wrong" to every person who will listen. Being in leadership requires making tough decisions. There are times when supporting staff underperform. There are times when people in our personal and professional circles take advantage of our kindness and the kindness of others around them. Many times, beneath the surface, these individuals are excessively needy or want us to give them the CliffsNotes version of our journeys. They often want the benefits of our journeys without making the sacrifices.

When these individuals are unable to charm or coerce us into giving them what they want, or into letting them take advantage of us or others, their next step is a smear campaign. They use insults, inferences, and innuendos to manipulate others into manipulating us. The intent is to turn the situation back on us. They attempt to enlist an audience of sympathizers to bully us into questioning our decisions. And they often use rumors to attract those sympathizers. Their intent is to convince us to second-guess our decisions and thinking, or to spend our waking hours reacting and responding to their foolishness.

In these cases, we are primed for them to destroy our plans and progress because we've compromised our thinking, and allowed ourselves to become distracted.

Instead, let us resist the temptation to explain our decisions to every person who inquires. Let us resist the temptation to try to reconcile with manipulative sharks. Let us avoid responding to rumors. Those who care about us and our calls will conclude that such rumors are none

**Encourage those sympathizers who carry their rumors and innuendos to also carry the burdens of their neediness, incompetencies, and entitlement.**

of their business, whether true or not. Those who entertain such rumors and innuendos are usually sharks as well.

Let us give ourselves *permission* to release those sharks to their sympathizers. Encourage those sympathizers who carry their rumors and innuendos to also carry the burdens of their neediness, incompetencies, and entitlement. It is easier to do so when we work at a high level of integrity. That way, sharks lose credibility immediately when they start spreading their false narratives. Let us keep the public informed of the positive work we are doing regularly. We can buffer the attacks of sharks, when we consistently build and stand by our brand.

## QUESTIONS FOR REFLECTION

1. Think of the situations when you encountered heckling sharks. How did you handle the situation? How much time did you spend processing the confrontation after it occurred? To what degree did the confrontation change your mood for the day?

2. In the heckling situation, now thinking back, would you have said less or more? Are there any things you would have said or done differently?

3. Do you observe that you are the target of hecklers more than other women with whom you work? If yes, why do you think that might be?

4. Think of the situations when you encountered manipulating sharks. Did their cries about your decisions make you second-guess yourself? Did you attempt to explain yourself? Why or why not?

5. How comfortable are you with dismissing manipulative sharks who prey on your kindness? If you are not very comfortable, how can you increase your comfort?

## CLOSING

Let us remember that many insults and rumors come from a place of insecurity. Those who are quick to point out what is wrong are often doing so in an attempt to deflect from their own wrongdoing. Do not catch the infections of insecurity, bitterness, or reactivity. It is best not to engage too much with sharks, whether the engagement is positive or negative. Instead, let us keep making the tough calls. Let us keep leading. Let us keep building. And let us keep sharks at a distance.

# Buffering the Shark Attacks

As women leaders, we are tasked with achieving a mission or fulfilling a call that no one sees, hears, or understands except us. It is challenging to lead people toward achieving a goal they have never conceived. When they haven't had the vision themselves, they will often devalue the mission, the call, the goal, and the tasks you have put into place.

That brings me to the shark attack of invalidation. Invalidation comes in many forms. Often, people pretend they do not see or understand the vision, mission, or call—even when they do. Others pretend they do not see or understand the value you bring to the table as a leader. Others pretend not to see progress when it is right in front of their very eyes.

Even when dealing with sharks, there is room for additional insight. As leaders, we often deal with the residual resentment of team members who have had very negative experiences with other employers. In their experiences, they have been invalidated. They are still suffering the wounds of sharks who have attacked them. They have not healed from a lack of transparency, coercion, co-opting of their ideas/contributions, or dismissals without cause. So often when working with supporting staff or those in authority over us, we are deemed guilty until proven innocent.

Unfortunately, *thank you*s come fewer and farther between than we would expect or appreciate. The gracious overtures and gestures we make are often regarded as if that is what we're supposed to do. We are often required to give loyalty to those who do not feel obligated to reciprocate such loyalty. As women, we are already subjected to pay discrepancies, but our salaries continue to be questioned, even when we provide the productivity of multiple people.

One thing I hope my readers take from this book is to understand that passive-aggressive attacks are still attacks. They are just as hurtful as overt attacks. Refusing to acknowledge the contributions of others is really no different than overtly saying the person brings no value to the table. Passive attacks should be acknowledged with equal weight to overt attacks, if we are to engage in the appropriate self-reflection that will lead to closure and making peace with what happens to us.

## QUESTIONS FOR REFLECTION

1. What contributions do you make to your professional context that you believe warrant acknowledgement and appreciation? Do you believe you receive the appropriate level of acknowledgement and appreciation? Why or why not?

2. What contributions do you make in your personal circles that you believe warrant acknowledgement and appreciation? Do you believe you receive the appropriate level of acknowledgement and appreciation? Why or why not?

3. If you do receive the appropriate level of acknowledgement and appreciation, how do you respond? Do you

return appreciation and acknowledgement with appreciation and acknowledgement?

4. If you do not receive the appropriate level of acknowledgement and appreciation, how do you respond? Do you keep it to yourself, or do you express your concern?

5. If you express concern, do you see meaningful steps to rectify the situation?

6. If you do not receive the appropriate level of appreciation and acknowledgement, how do you affirm yourself?

## CLOSING

While working among sharks, and sometimes living among sharks, we should come to expect a lack of gratitude. But let us not become overly focused on the unkind tendencies of sharks. Instead we can celebrate the expressions we do receive. Someone saying "thank you" is definitely an overt expression. Let us not forget the support we receive for our visions and our calls. A warm smile goes a long way. But we should also give ourselves *permission* to appreciate *ourselves.*

Sometimes the passive-aggressive tendencies of sharks help us grow beyond the temptation to seek external validation. These negative experiences are sometimes the catalyst we need to set our own metrics for success and fulfillment. We then give ourselves *permission* to follow through and can then forget about it. We then give ourselves *permission* to set metrics for creating and maintaining our peace. We give ourselves *permission* to set metrics for enjoying life outside of our occupations or organizations. And ultimately, we can give ourselves *permission* to celebrate every benchmark met!

# Embrace Being Underestimated

Sometimes sharks purposefully invalidate us with the intention of making us feel unqualified and unworthy. But other times the people in our personal and professional circles are oblivious to our capabilities and contributions. They are oblivious often because they have come to expect that women cannot be capable of competence in or make valuable contributions to certain areas. We work and live in a world that, more often than not, projects some type of inferiority onto women who answer the call to make their own mark on the world.

I learned how to embrace being underestimated from my mother. My mother rarely divulges the extent of her legacy. Her family has deep roots in social justice and civil rights, which are recorded in Alabama's historical documents. One day, I asked her, "Why don't you tell people about your lineage and family legacy?"

She replied, "Because I prefer to be underestimated."

People are more likely to divulge information about themselves when they underestimate us. That's how we learn which doors may be available to us. We can seize the opportunity to maneuver through doors and into spaces that were not designed for us in the first place. That is when the sharks waiting for us do not see us coming. And thus, we can take advantage of opening a number of doors before the sharks have the opportunity to attack. Being underestimated can give us the chance to create, access, and leverage valuable opportunities the sharks never saw coming!

## QUESTIONS FOR REFLECTION

1. In what ways do you feel underestimated in your personal life? In what ways do you feel underestimated in your professional life?

2. Who benefits from you being underestimated? Are the beneficiaries underestimating you directly, or are there other players with whom you have more direct conflict?

3. Are those people underestimating you in your personal and professional circles blocking you from decision makers or advocates who can help you fulfill your call? How can you use such underestimation to bring you closer to those individuals who can help advance progress toward your call?

## CLOSING

Part of protecting and keeping our peace involves finding ways to see opportunities in our struggles. We must continuously buffer the sharks in our personal and professional spaces by finding ways to reframe their attacks. In the reframing, we are less likely to internalize the ill intent or ill results, so we can maintain the necessary energy to fulfill our calls. We must give ourselves *permission* to reject all forms of invalidation, while still using those hurtful actions to work for our good.

# Working With versus Building With

Women—in our work, sometimes we cannot control the sharks in our professional circles. Working with those who do not share our values, ways of being, beliefs, and ways of community is inevitable.

As we navigate those circles and work to preserve our mental well-being, one helpful principle is discerning between the people we are *working with* and those who we are *building with*. Being able to make this distinction has been a helpful strategy to denying sharks access to kill and destroy.

As a social entrepreneur, a CEO, or a leader, we often must hire employees or retain employees who, at the time, are not a long-term fit for the organization. These are the people we *work with*. Sometimes it takes a while to determine if a person is a fit for your organization or circle. Here are some behaviors we can watch for, which help us determine whether a person is one we will want to work with or build with.

Workers glaze over and change the subject when we talk about vision and strategy. Builders plug in, become enthusiastic, and exchange ideas that can help bring the vision to fruition. Workers avoid immersion in the work and the circle of people who truly carries out the work. Builders take instruction, ask follow-up questions to better understand the concept to which they're contributing, and come to observe other parts of the organization that their tasks impact. Workers ask *why* to see how the work can be steered to their convenience. Builders ask *why* to determine how their work can advance the overall vision. Workers are quick to complain. Builders are quick to problem solve.

## QUESTIONS FOR REFLECTION

1.  Take some time to list those people in your professional and personal circles who you work with. List those you believe you can build with. What criteria did you use to distinguish between your workers and builders?

2. How much of your discretionary work and personal time do you spend with "workers"? How much of your discretionary work and personal time do you spend with "builders"? Do you see any imbalances? Why or why not?

3. How much information about your vision and call do you share with workers? How much do you share with builders? Do you see any imbalances? Why or why not?

4. Do you need to make any adjustments to the amount of time and information you are sharing with workers? Do you need to make any adjustments to the amount of time and information you are sharing with builders? How are you going to go about making those adjustments? How will you address the resistance?

## CLOSING

Sometimes, workers are the last to move on, even when it's clear they are not a fit for our organizations. One of the ways we can manage frustration is by giving ourselves *permission* to believe that these individuals only need to be here for a season. Workers can continue to carry out functions while they are still a part of the organization, but we do not have to include them as part of the building process. Once we give ourselves *permission* to not include workers in the activities of builders, then our conversations with employees, colleagues, partnering organizations, and other groups become more focused, intentional, productive, and hopefully less frustrating. We stop wasting time and effort explaining overall strategy to those who were not interested in building along with us in the first place. And we protect our peace by refusing to invest emotional energy into those who are not interested in building either.

# Run Your Race: Focus on *Your* Call!

I continue to observe that verbal attacks, sabotage, and other acts of aggression sharks unleash against women leaders are often designed to make us forfeit our calls. Those persistent, seemingly petty attacks make us feel as if we are dying of a million paper cuts. Either we give up in discouragement, or we do not perform to our potential because we are burdened with emotions related to how we are treated. Over time, if we are not careful, those acts diminish our sense of self to the point where we have disengaged from our calls altogether.

One of the most common tactics I see is comparison. It is best that we refuse to engage in conversations that compare individuals or groups to one another. Comparisons suggest there is one standard we all should achieve to the detriment of our uniqueness. When we strive to match an external standard, we compromise our authenticity. Comparisons also catalyze competition. Where there is competition, there is a temptation to withdraw in defeat, resort to destructive measures to get an advantage, or assume false complacency because we feel like we have "won" for the moment.

Here is one of the ways we can deal with the destructive nature of comparisons: we run our own races in our own lanes. We focus on our own calls! There can't be a competition if we refuse to participate. We can simply say, "That's great," "That's nice," or "That's amazing," and then ask the person making the comparisons or instigating the competitive questions about how they are advancing their own call. We can challenge those sharks to dig in introspectively to find a focus, rather than creating misery or unnecessary angst.

And finally, we can protect our peace by working that much harder to fulfill our own individual calls. When we are intentionally and authentically fulfilling our individual calls, we exude a joy that is infectious to those who are positive. That same joy is repelling to those sharks who are negative, destructive, or out of touch with their own calls.

## QUESTIONS FOR REFLECTION

1. In what areas of your life do you feel you do not yet "measure up"? How did you come to that conclusion? Did you compare yourself to someone else?

2. How do you handle conversations that center around comparison? Do you listen? Do you continue the conversation? How much of your discretionary time do you spend engaging in such conversations?

3. How do you feel when comparison conversations come to a close? Are you usually the one who feels unworthy or less capable, or do you tend to come out on top?

4. How can you steer your personal and professional culture from comparison conversations?

## CLOSING

Rather than spending our valuable time comparing ourselves to others, let us spend more time cultivating the value of authentic preparation for what we are called to do. Instead let us do the internal work we need to do so we have the wisdom, depth, substance, and maturity to fulfill our calls and attain those things we want in life. My mother used to always

**You do not want to lose your mind trying to gain or hold on to what you think you want.**

emphasize mental preparation and say, "You do not want to lose your mind trying to gain or hold on to what you think you want." Even if we come out on top of the comparisons today, there will always be others who can quickly eclipse all we have attained and earned. Let us give ourselves *permission* to follow our paths to the end without the distraction of comparisons. That is where we are able to find and keep peace.

# Saving Face Saves No One

Another critical strategy in keeping peace is doing regular internal assessments of how we work and interact in both our personal and professional circles. This is the building block to accountability. However, when we are not at peace or in authentic alignment with our call, we can find ourselves taking on projects, ideas, and paths that were never for us in the first place. And when we do, we run the risk of underperforming or blurring ethical lines.

When that happens, the best thing we can do is take responsibility for our actions. We should acknowledge the shortcomings and find a way to rectify the situation. This sets us apart from those people who have not done the internal work that allows them to face their own shortcomings. Those who cannot face their own shortcomings tend to devise excessive excuses, point fingers, become indignant, and spend unnecessary time trying to find inconsistencies in everyone else to justify their lack of performance or ethics. Rather than face the issue, they use these tactics to "save face." Unfortunately, the situation becomes muddier, and it ends up being a long, wide road of confusion and conflict. And in most cases, the excuses and deflections leave them no less exposed. It only creates an ugly and dysfunctional work environment.

We must be on alert for those who try to save face. When pressed for accountability, they can often turn into sharks. They will attack our character and our competence in order to deflect from their lack of performance or ethics.

## QUESTIONS FOR REFLECTION

1. When you make a mistake, how easy is it for you to acknowledge it?

2. If it is not easy for you to acknowledge a mistake, why is that? What experiences have contributed to your discomfort with acknowledging mistakes?

3. Is it easy or difficult for you to hold others accountable when they underperform? Do you find yourself helping them save face? If so, what experiences have shaped your tendency to help people save face?

4. For those who find it easier to hold underperformers accountable, how do you communicate with the underperforming person? Do you find the resolution comes quickly, or does it lag? Do the communications become more negative and entangled over time? What steps do you take to hold underperformers accountable and bring the solution to resolution?

5. When you underperform, how do you rectify the situation?

## CLOSING

When we encounter those who would rather save face, do not indulge them. We should stick to the issue at hand. We should avoid value judgements and assessments of intentions and focus on the indicators of underperformance or nonperformance. We should give each party the opportunity to bring performance to an acceptable level, and if possible, work with them to further refine expectations. If we are able, then we should also provide them with capacity and resources that can help them perform better. If there is a mutually agreed upon fee, and such capacity exceeds those costs/commitments, then we can certainly point them to resources that can help them avoid such issues in the future.

If in fact, we are the ones who have underperformed or not performed at all, let us give ourselves *permission* to make mistakes. Sometimes, we take on more work than we can manage. Sometimes we trust the wrong people to carry out critical functions. Sometimes life happens, and we need to recalibrate. Whatever the reason, when we give ourselves *permission* to make mistakes or fall short, then we can take *responsibility*, make *improvements*, and learn the necessary lessons. When we can create positive resolutions, then we can maintain our peace.

# Peace and Solitude

As important as togetherness and belonging can be, embracing solitude is a critical component in both protecting against sharks and keeping our peace. Sharks circle the waters and often mobilize in a pack when we stand up for ourselves or our convictions. They often attack through exclusion or insult, which can be a sign it's a good time for you to retreat for a while. When we find ourselves consistently experiencing resistance and rejection, sometimes that means our gifts are not on display for the right audience. It may be a signal that we need to step away, reflect a little more, and potentially refine our ideas and strategies for a bigger and better audience. When we are sensitive to the signs, we can use rejection as a means to embrace solitude. In solitude, we can recharge, rethink, refine, and revitalize. We can often re-emerge with a stronger plan than ever before!

For women, it can be hard to embrace solitude. We are conditioned to "belong." Even when we engage in relaxing activities, we find our minds wandering to figure out if everyone else is okay. We are conditioned to *share*—share our accomplishments, share our talents, share our abilities, share ourselves with *everybody*.

It can also be a challenge to figure out how to reclaim our private space. For those of us with families, it is even more difficult. We try to balance the necessary nurturance of children, partners, and aging parents with the nurturance of ourselves. As there are often unanticipated events and factors we cannot control, we are tempted to abandon preplanning of the things that we *can* control.

Though I have no children of my own, I played an integral role in caring for my niece, who is now twelve. I cared for her from the time she was eight months old. I set up a room for her in my home, and it was me and her! I remember moving into my first purchased home when she was two, and I brought her by to approve it. She ran all through the space proclaiming it was "*our* home." She was a very well-adjusted child; however, she was an only child who required meaningful engagement.

It was difficult managing an infant, toddler, and preschooler while building a nonprofit, working on a PhD, and teaching part time at a university. At the time, I managed dual residences in dual cities. It was difficult managing myself! I had to embrace a system, and I decided to reduce my social time, so I could love on my niece, stay focused, and prepare myself to answer the call.

I also recognized early that the key to developing and maintaining a support system is having a routine. I established a schedule we followed consistently. Within that schedule, I was careful to analyze and monitor the time devoted to answering my call and self-care. I planned self-care activities as a method to prepare for the demands of the week. For example, I purchased clothing for myself and my niece in common colors, to ease the burden of laundering. I set certain days for laundering and then put outfits together as I hung them up. That way, they were ready for my niece and me to grab as we started our days. I planned meals carefully by selecting meals that would yield at least one extra day of leftovers or that could be converted into lunches. In some instances, I could drop her off with meals already prepared. I would use my Crock Pot on Sundays to ensure we were ahead of the demands of the week. I also ensured my niece operated on a routine of rest, structured time for fun, and structured time for quiet, as to not overburden those who would have to support me with her. Our routine gave our support system a structure they could add to and supplement, at their convenience. Meaning—although I had a support system, the responsibility was still mine whenever my niece was with me.

## QUESTIONS FOR REFLECTION

1. How many hours do you spend weekly in solitude? That means *alone*, and alone with your thoughts, without distraction.

2. Is your discretionary time in solitude intentional, or is it a result of some other factor? If so, what is the factor that contributes to your time spent in solitude?

3. Do you embrace or resist solitude? If you embrace solitude, what experiences shape that tendency? If you resist solitude, what experiences may have shaped your resistance to solitude?

4. What do you do with the time you spend in solitude? Do you relax? Do you engage in creative activities?

5. What steps can you take to ensure you're able to spend more time in solitude? What steps can you take to ensure your time in solitude contributes to the amount of peace you feel within yourself?

## CLOSING

We must give ourselves *permission* to embrace solitude. Solitude gives us the opportunity to sit with our emotions. We can acknowledge the shark attacks that hurt us.

We can acknowledge the disappointments we've encountered. We can anticipate and process current and anticipated shark attacks. However, we must not use solitude to only analyze what has hurt us. We should also use the time to celebrate our wins. We should use this time to cultivate creativity and to foster expectancy for fulfilling our calls. But remember, we must also devote time in solitude to doing nothing, nothing at all. Let us not forget that peace also involves us giving ourselves *permission* to just *be*!

# Key Points to Remember

- We are more successful in navigating sharks when we are able to identify them and leverage their tendencies to our advantage. We know sharks may work with and for us, but they will never help us build. They will use a series of overt and passive tactics to block us, hurt us, and discourage us. But if we refuse to waste time engaging with them or entering their spaces, and instead use their underestimations to move through doors they would never suspect we were moving toward, then we can reach our goals despite them.

- Comparisons do not inspire anyone to be better or do better. When we focus on only our own calls, we see attributes in others that inspire us. We fare much better when we seek to learn from others and draw out those attributes that are more relevant to our calls, rather than using others as a measuring stick to define who we are and whether we are hitting the mark.

- We save time and headaches when we resist the temptation to save face. It matters more how we conduct ourselves than how we appear at any given time.

- If we are going to experience any peace while carrying out our calls, we must intentionally plan time and space for solitude and silence. It is in these times when we can process hurt and triumph, while creating new opportunities for the future. But remember, we must also plan for quiet space to simply exist and be. It is in those times when we replenish, restore, and reset.

# Elevation in Action

Take some time to list all the sharks and place their names under the following categories:

- Sharks I can avoid.

- Sharks I must confront.

- Sharks I can leverage.

Devise a strategy for how you will address sharks in each category. Will you avoid them by not entering their spaces, or not inviting them into your spaces or conversations? Will you intentionally develop a plan to disengage from communication? For sharks you must confront, how will you lead with principles, ethics, and the specific issues while sharks are trying to interfere with your call? Are there other allies you can enlist for support? How will you leverage those sharks that underestimate you? In what areas can you begin navigating right around them?

Also develop a written schedule of your week and be sure to add no less than thirty minutes daily for solitude. If you are only able to devote thirty minutes, begin with a focus on just "being." Make a list of resources or supports that can facilitate your peaceful solitude. Select a regular location so your mind knows it's time to relax and simply be. Then, add an additional thirty minutes each day, if at all possible, to engage in something nonwork related that gives you joy. If you are not able to devote thirty minutes daily, try to find two hours weekly to relax, reset, and maintain your peace.

CHAPTER 4

# *LEADING WITH LOVE*

Overcoming obstacles often requires fighting for survival. It seems like a daily grind that does not end. But in fighting for survival, we also manage internal struggles. We must resist the temptation to allow bitterness to sink in. We have to discern between what's in our right to do, what is in our best interest, and what is in the best interest of the organization we are leading.

Part of managing these conflicts is giving ourselves permission to "lead with love." Leading with love may seem weak to those who have not learned the art. But leading with love also makes us vulnerable, relatable, and attractive to those who are mission/call-minded. Leading with love helps us develop skills for gathering consensus and mobilizing others to make a greater impact than what we would be able to do alone. Finally, leading with love keeps us positive. It allows us to actually enjoy the journey we are on—with its twists and turns.

Critical to leading with love is knowing our "why" and making sure our "why" runs deeper than the situation before us at the time. When we lead with love, we think about more than our immediate self-interests. We think about the people we impact. We think about how what we do can make a tangible difference. And in a world that seems to promote self-serving behavior, those who lead with love stand out that much taller. Yes—there is a way to promote the greater good and reap the benefits of an authentic, lasting, positive brand.

# Mission before "the Shine"

One of the ways we can lead with love and serve in the face of adversity and hostility is by focusing on *doing* impactful deeds rather than trying to *be* impactful. When we focus on trying to *be* impactful, we run the risk of diverting the attention that should be reserved for those we are serving onto ourselves. And when the focus diverts from those we serve onto ourselves, we can compromise our authenticity and ultimately our joy and power. Focusing on *being* impactful can also make us more vulnerable to the negative opinions of others and their invalidations. When we focus on *being* impactful and do not receive the recognition we believe we deserve, we present an opportunity for bitterness to set in.

When we lead with love, we focus on *doing* the work. When we are focused on *doing* the work, we are less likely to notice the smallness of our detractors. And when we are presented with hostility, we can process it, dismiss it, and then move on. When we focus on *doing* impactful things, we don't put a value judgment on that impact. If a word, deed, or listening ear makes a bright spot in our lives or anyone else's life, then it is a cause to rejoice. In other words, the small wins are just as sweet! We can savor those because we know we are moving one step closer to fulfilling our calls.

## QUESTIONS FOR REFLECTION

1. List your top five goals in life. How many of them relate to something you want to accomplish? How many of them relate to a title, recognition, or an asset you want to attain? How many relate to something you can do to help advance the goals/dreams of others?

2. After categorizing your goals, are you satisfied with the mix of goals? Do you believe there are any imbalances between goals related to *being* impactful, when compared to *doing* impactful things?

3. Consider your progress toward your goals. Are you making the level of progress toward your goals you would like? Are you making more progress toward goals related to *being* impactful or *doing* impactful things?

4. Do you see any relationships between your state of mind/ peace and your progress toward *being* impactful? Do you see any relationships between your state of mind/peace and *doing* impactful things?

5. If you are not satisfied with the mix of goals related to *being* impactful compared to *doing* impactful things, what changes can you make?

## CLOSING

From a marketing perspective, there are many trends upon which we can capitalize to build a business and be successful. If we want, we can work hard enough and establish the appropriate relationships to receive external recognitions and validations. However, the world is starving for kindness. There are so many opportunities to *do impactful work*, which can support you financially while feeding your soul. If you see an imbalance and want to invest more energy in *doing* impactful things but are not sure how, broaden your definitions of impact and broaden your territories. Give yourself *permission* to pursue opportunities and spaces where you can lead with love as opposed to leading for an agenda.

> **Give yourself *permission* to pursue opportunities and spaces where you can lead with love as opposed to leading for an agenda.**

# Humility and Gratitude

Another way we can prepare ourselves to lead with love is by intentionally operating with humility and gratitude. I'll share one thing I try to do every morning when I wake up. I meditate on the days prior to receiving some of the blessings I hold dear. There were many days of struggle and many scars. Meditating on those days of struggle keeps us humble and grateful. It helps us treat our direct and indirect reports graciously.

Humility reminds us to forgive as we have been forgiven. More often than we realize, we've inadvertently spoken and acted insensitively. In those situations, we are unaware of the impact because someone chose to forgive. We benefit from mercy, not fully reaping the consequences for situations mishandled. We experience grace, reaping blessings we don't deserve. We are able to more effectively galvanize others around an issue or a call when we are empathic. We are more empathic when we make a conscious effort to remember our own days of struggle.

Gratitude helps us lead with love because we refrain from taking any blessing or act of kindness for granted. Life brings about so many transitions. Laughter can quickly turn to tears. Dollars, titles, and assets can dissolve right before our eyes. We can lose those we love, and the relationships we cherish can be damaged beyond repair.

Humility and gratitude help us enjoy the blessings and edifying relationships that surround us. Remember—ultimately, we are here to build a life. If we're not careful, we can attain everything we believe we want and yet remain miserable. We disincentivize good people who wish to support us because we fail to acknowledge or appreciate their love and kindness. But when we operate with gratitude, we are able to uplift the efforts of those who support our vision and who want to help us advance our call. We can then spend more time lifting what is right rather than complaining about what is wrong. As a result, we are more likely to build excitement about what we are endeavoring to do and mobilize authentic support.

## QUESTIONS FOR REFLECTION

1. List five experiences personally or professionally you believe give you the sensitivity you need to lead with love.

2. List five positive experiences you've had in the last week you are grateful for. Did you communicate your gratitude to

those who contributed to those positive experiences? Why or why not?

3. After thinking about those positive experiences and the contributors, what steps can you take to engage them more in helping you to fulfill your call?

## CLOSING

Some are quick to associate joy, humility, and gratitude for denial or escaping reality. Instead, consider an attitude of humility and gratitude as an act of resistance. There are forces designed to steal joy, peace, confidence, and our entire mental well-being. There are others who listen and read carefully to find, fuel, and exploit our vulnerabilities. The small things we take for granted are often enviable to a person on the outside looking in. Someone else might be waiting for the opportunity to take that blessing, which in times of frustration, we might deem a curse. Rather than hand any opportunities to my enemies, let us allow humility and gratitude to put the challenges, struggles, and annoyances into perspective. That way we refrain from using up our strength unnecessarily. And then we are able to fight the most important battles.

Hard times will come. Relationships will be tested. Don't forget to pause and breathe. List what is going right, and balance that against the issue at hand. When we operate with gratitude and humility, we can further lead with love, because we are better able to weigh when to speak and when to listen. We can better weigh whether to think or whether to act. Leading with love, humility, and gratitude saves us guilt, as it gives us no reason to speak in anger, frustration, or haste. And finally, leading with love, humility, and gratitude gives us *permission* and the freedom to forgive!

# Leading with Graciousness

As we prepare for potentially stressful situations, let us resist the temptation to state the negative and hurtful obvious, especially when we know our comments will not bring about any meaningful and positive change. Being gracious is essential to leading with love. When we are gracious, we make it a point to speak and act in ways that do not make others feel small or inadequate.

When we lead with love, we are gracious, even when graciousness is not extended to us. We are able to be gracious to others even when they confuse such kindness and class with naïvete. We treat people with the dignity they deserve, even when it's not the level of dignity they are accustomed to. We speak life into people even when they are too insecure to speak life back into us. We support others' gifts. We invest in others' dreams. We support people without judgment. We fill in the gaps to help them grow and do so *quietly*. If they refuse to accept or respect our graciousness, we move on in peace.

Leading with love and graciousness can be quite a challenge sometimes. It can be difficult to operate in a space of healing when we're constantly being hurt. However, returning "hurt for hurt" rarely helps anyone. We all end up wounded.

So, during those times when we're tempted to throw graciousness out the window, let us remember that the following actions typically cannot be done *at the same time.*

- We cannot create consensus and catalyze conflict.

- We cannot build and destroy.

- We cannot command respect and dish out disrespect— not even "dressed up" in what appears to be "professional" language or tone.

## QUESTIONS FOR REFLECTION

1. What situations or which people trigger you to throw graciousness out the window?

2. Do you know what actions and words could perhaps bring out the best in the people who trigger you the most? How can you use grace to turn the tables and switch the atmosphere from negative to positive?

3. Are you afraid of being vulnerable? If so, why? What opportunities might lie ahead if you were willing to take the chance of being hurt, in the interest of giving grace to others?

> We can look in the mirror and love the woman we see. We can aim for the stars and not someone's jugular. Aiming for the stars takes us farther anyway.

## CLOSING

When we lead with love and graciousness, no matter how we are treated, we can sleep at night in peace. Treating others with graciousness is also evidence that we love ourselves. The words and deeds of others do not possess the power to shift our moods or ways of being. And thus, we can look at ourselves in the mirror and continue to love the woman we see. Therefore, we can continue to aim for the stars and not someone's jugular. Aiming for the stars usually takes us farther in the long run, anyway.

# The "One Up" Takes Us Down

Leading with love also involves resisting the temptation to compete with those who we feel have been gifted with positions over us that they don't deserve. Sometimes it is hard to accept when we believe someone is "sitting in our seat." And, sometimes, if we are not careful, resentment shows up through passive-aggressive actions such as:

1. Trying to show up another colleague or superior by presenting information that undermines their competency. For example, exploiting what we deem to be contradictions or oversights and magnifying them.

2. Exploiting soft spots in their lives. For example, consistently highlighting our relationship status when we have heard our colleague or superior is struggling in that area. Or constantly harping upon healthy eating, working out, or one's dress size when our colleague or superior has concerns about their weight or other aspects of their appearance.

3. Sabotaging their projects and advancement. For example, knowingly leaving out details, information, or tasks that would purposely cause that person to fail.

4. Undermining their reputation through spreading rumors and hurtful innuendos.

Sometimes, we feel if we can show up the person in front of us, we will get noticed. And we believe being noticed will put us in a position to elevate professionally. Unfortunately, that rarely happens.

Why? Because attacking our superiors or colleagues casts us in a much more negative light than the one we're trying to project. Why? Attacking others because they have what we think we want suggests we are not ready to fill those shoes anyway. When we think that we can exploit minor oversights or contradictions of others, it shows we do not understand the magnitude of what it takes to move to the next level. Those who have been elevated to new levels of responsibility are required to manage across departments and systems. Focusing on details is no longer their highest priority. They are often called to engage in higher-level thinking on issues that could not be disclosed to us anyway. So, when we are quick to critique and expose, we're actually demonstrating we are not capable of the conversations, responsibilities, or challenges that come with the position we want.

Second, when we decide to compete within our organizations, we are also showing that we are thinking too small. It often reveals we believe our only opportunities are within the context of where we work, right now. Instead of wounding one another until all our reputations are damaged beyond repair, let us instead open our minds beyond the current situation and look for an environment where we do not have to fight to be seen.

## QUESTIONS FOR REFLECTION

1. Do you believe there is anyone in the way of you moving to the next level of fulfilling your call? How long has that person been in the way? What kind of working relationship do you have with that person?

2. How easy is it for you to allow issues to work out on their own? Do you believe you are the one who has to expose inconsistencies or oversights? Why is that?

3. How much time are you diverting from fulfilling *your* call, when you spend time looking for and exploiting the lack of competency in others?

4. Are there opportunities to learn from those who we do not like, or those we feel have been given what we believe we deserve?

## CLOSING

Instead of focusing on what others have and what they are doing, let us take that valuable time to be introspective. Let us revisit what we truly want and why we want it. Then let us give ourselves *permission* to dream and explore beyond our present environment. If we are not being appreciated or promoted in our current workplace, then let us be honest with ourselves about the probability that such a culture will change. If competition, exploitation, and sabotage can get us what we want, then what will happen when someone else wants what we have?

In order to be successful, it is more important for us to analyze what we want to accomplish and look at the required skills rather than at the person who possesses success now. We need to study what the next level entails. What are the challenges? What are the responsibilities? What types of interpersonal skills will be essential? What can we learn from those we do not like, or those who we believe have the position we deserve? Do they possess skills and experiences maybe we haven't considered? How can we leverage the opportunity to learn from them and about them, and how can we get where they are?

Then the next step is to start developing the skills necessary for leadership, regardless of when and where it happens. As we see ourselves as learners who do not have all the answers, it makes it easier for us to understand others who are still using the wrong methods to get to the right outcome. And that allows us to lead and work with love, building the reputation and foundation not only to elevate our position—but to fulfill our calls.

# Loving the Ones You Lead

When we are tasked with leading organizations or departments, it is draining work. We find ourselves fatigued on some days to the point of feeling physically paralyzed. In those moments, it is tempting for us to over-rely on our direct reports to fill in the gaps. Some of the ways we do so is by asking our reports to perform tasks outside of their job descriptions that are of personal convenience to us but do not necessarily advance the mission of the organizations we are leading. This should not be confused with asking individuals to give extra effort, as we give extra effort to make sure the mission or vision is carried out. This also should not be confused with delegating tasks so we can focus more heavily on advancing the mission and enhancing the work environment/quality of service for all. Instead, we should refrain from

- asking or allowing reports to perform personal services for us (picking up meals, making calls, managing our schedules/ other tasks, taking notes) if these tasks are not in their job description.

- using our authority to coerce reports to handle contentious/difficult situations/calls unless this is a part of their job description.

- requiring direct reports to listen to our problems, frustrations, and other personal issues.

- allowing those inside or outside our organizations to engage in personal services (cleaning, childcare, running errands), unless they are contracted to do so, and there is a specific job description and defined hours.

## QUESTIONS FOR REFLECTION

1.  Who do you call on when you feel overwhelmed? Are they a direct report? How often do you call on them? What sorts of things do you ask them to do?

2.  How do those people on whom you lean respond? Are they happy to help, or do you sense any hesitancy?

3.  When you're leaning on them for support, how could you potentially distract them from fulfilling their calls? What responsibilities are they failing to assume so they can support you?

## CLOSING

When we lean on others as a natural reaction to our stress and fatigue, we must take the time to consider how our requests are impacting them. We must consider that those who report to us, or those who are around us, also have responsibilities, stressors, and lives too. They may not have the capacity to take on our baggage, even if there is a paid opportunity to do so. When we are not considerate of those who report to us, we foster resentment. Also be aware of the possibility that as people assume activities outside of their job description, they are neglecting tasks that are critical to their job description. When we take too much from one area, we stand to lose in a valuable area. Therefore, let us continue to lead with love, love on those who report to us, and understand the dividends that leading with love pays.

# Leading with Love and Letting Things Slide

When we lead with love, we must resist the temptation to give our supporting team members a pass when it is not warranted. Sometimes we are tempted to do so because we see they are not our worst team members. But when we let things slide, we are actually admitting defeat at the onset. We have already conceded that the situation cannot improve and the department or organization we lead cannot do any better. Or we have traded in our authority and self-respect to be liked or accepted by the people we have been tasked to lead.

Leaders cannot be hesitant to enforce quality standards or policies. When there is a violation, one of the worst things we can do is avoid addressing it. Why? Because our reports pick up on the areas in which we are hesitant to enforce accountability, and they often seize the moment to escalate those violations. The violations can escalate to the point where we are putting either our job on the line, or the jobs of innocent people who had nothing to do with the situation. In our information society, mistakes and lapses in judgment can be readily accessed, keeping us from recovering, starting over, or promoting.

How do we resist the temptation? We must think bigger! When we make decisions, we must look beyond the present situation. We must refuse to slip into survival mode even when things get hard. If we proceed with ethics, competency, and consistency, we *will* survive. When we make decisions and encounter violations in policies or quality standards, we must view the present as the foundation for the future.

## QUESTIONS FOR REFLECTION

1. In what areas of your organization are you tempted to let violations in procedures or quality standards slide?

2. Who could be negatively impacted by you choosing to continue letting violations in procedures and/or quality standards slide?

3. If your department/organization doubled, tripled, or quadrupled in size and personnel, would you be able to let those same violations slide? Why or why not?

4. If you were promoted to supervise more supervisors or train other trainers, would you be able to let those same violations slide? Why or why not?

## CLOSING

Before we decide to let violations slide, let us start thinking less about protecting the violators and more about protecting those who support us personally, as well as our abilities to fulfill our calls. Let us think more about how our decisions impact those who have granted us the opportunity to lead. In letting things slide, are we violating their trust? By letting things slide, are we exposing them in a way that could cost them their job or reputation? By letting things slide, are we creating unnecessary stress for the ones who have trusted us with responsibility, by requiring them to step in and make tough choices we should be making ourselves? How does letting things slide impact the financial health of our organizations? Does letting things slide cost the organization customers or revenue? Does letting things slide increase the expenses of the organization?

How do we resist temptation? By giving ourselves *permission* to think bigger! When we make decisions, we must look beyond the present situation. We must refuse to slip into survival mode even when things get hard. If we proceed with ethics, competency, and consistency, we *will* survive. When we make decisions and encounter violations in policies or quality standards, we must view the present as the foundation for the future.

> **We must look beyond the present and refuse to slip into survival mode when things get hard. We must view the present as the foundation for the future.**

Instead, let us start leading as if our departments/organizations have grown exponentially *right now*! Otherwise, we will be running around, covering up unnecessary fires until we no longer can. We will continue to recycle unproductive employees until the productivity of our departments/organizations is questioned or our capacity to grow our departments/organizations is questioned. When we get to this point, the next question will be if *we* are worth the organization's investment. Let *no one* pull you down this path! The crown is heavy, but we accepted it. Let us breathe, brace ourselves, put our crowns on and wear them well!

# Key Points to Remember

- Though we continue to struggle and fight to overcome the obstacles designed to keep us from fulfilling our call, we must resist the temptation to return evil for evil. Matching evil for evil is a full-time job in and of itself. It closes the door to enlisting the advocates and mentors who can help us advance our calls. Adopting an evil-for-evil way of being makes situations messier. It becomes difficult to legitimize our competence and work when we resort to petty, nasty discourse and actions.

- When we lead with love, we give ourselves *permission* to move forward with our eyes to the future, rather than over our shoulders.

- As we move to the next chapter, let us remember we can more easily lead with love when we are mission motivated and not self-serving.

- Humility and gratitude give us the capacity to lead with love because we are more likely to remember the areas in which we need or have needed to grow. Aiming for the stars and not the jugular keeps us focused on our own capacities for growth and leads to us fulfilling our calls much more effectively.

- When we lead with sensitivity and do not drain the capacities of those who report to us, we are much more likely to lead them in advancing the missions of our organizations.

- But remember, leading with love never means letting things slide. Accountability is a part of growth.

## *Elevation* in Action

In closing this chapter, I leave you with a challenge.

1. Name one to two people who are helping you advance your organization's mission/fulfill your call. List three intentional

ways you can highlight and uplift their contributions/ achievements.

2. List three ways you can respond to those who negatively trigger you without undermining their dignity/self-respect.

3. List three activities that your direct reports are doing that are not in their job description and develop a strategy to take those tasks off their plates. If the people performing extra tasks are not in your organization, list how you will structure the relationship and compensate them.

4. Devise a strategy to address violations in your organization/ department and hold the proper individuals accountable.

CHAPTER 5

# PERMISSION TO FIGHT, PERMISSION TO OVERCOME!

In this book we've discussed ways to lead peaceably and to lead with love. However, there will be times where fighting will be inevitable. Our most valuable weapon is our mind. As women, we are conditioned and sometimes even programmed to avoid confrontation at all costs. We are often pressured to become passive victims who are assaulted and given no voice. I wrote this poem, "Feminine Fighters," in the hopes that we will give ourselves *permission* to fight for our brands, fight for our principles, fight to fulfill our calls, fight to overcome!

## Feminine Fighters

*Love is patient, love is kind;*

*love is a lot of things, but love is not blind!*

*Women can be servants, women can nurture,*

*but women can also lead; women can be warriors!*

*You can be humble and still be confident.*

*Let no one limit your dreams; you always have options!*

*It doesn't matter if people acknowledge, support, or agree with what you do,*

*you will always find satisfaction when to yourself, you are true!*

# Defending against Dream Stealers

For those of us in business, analyzing threats is a part of how we build our business plans, as well as test the soundness of our plans. We cannot afford to lead unaware of the threats that can distract us, derail us from, or destroy the call we are trying to fulfill. However, maintaining vigilance, zeal, and joy can be a challenge. But remember this—for every threat we encounter, we learn valuable lessons and become stronger as we fight to survive.

One type of threat we often encounter is dream stealers. Dream stealers copy, imitate, and try to profit from our ideas and contributions. They are often individuals who try to talk us out of our dreams, or discourage us, just to co-opt the dreams for themselves. Or they are the type of people who sabotage us to keep the dream from being realized in the first place.

Whereas we must be cognizant of dream stealers, we must refuse to obsess about people who reject us, try to knock us off our "thrones," or attempt to imitate the work we are doing. While we must be aware of internal and external threats, we must remember that if we look down too long, then we can't look forward. And in refusing to look forward, we miss the rich opportunities to fulfill our calls, which are right in front of our eyes.

**For every threat we encounter, we learn valuable lessons and become stronger as we fight to survive.**

So let us not become discouraged when we see others attempting to imitate our work or attempting to build on our foundation for their personal gain or recognition. As infuriating as imitators can be, remember, they are imitating the revelations we have already received. And if they are imitating what we have already created/discovered, then that leaves us the space to continue creating new products/insights/opportunities. Imitators are an indicator we are on the right path, but they also remind us we still have more calls to fulfill.

Also remember, if someone can duplicate overnight what it has taken us years to develop and accomplish, know that the test of production will be the fire that will destroy the imitation as quickly as it was built. If they are incapable of developing the product/service/idea, then they will not be able to implement it or apply it across contexts. Rather, we can be consoled by the fact that we are attracting so many imitators because we make it look easy!

## QUESTIONS FOR REFLECTION

1. What dreams do you have that are constantly discouraged by others around you? Which people do we find discouraging us the most?

2. How do you respond when someone imitates your idea, professionally or personally?

3. How much time do we spend processing our emotions when our ideas are imitated?

## CLOSING

When our ideas are imitated, we can rest in the assurance that we are still on the cutting edge. And instead of being discouraged, we can use our gift of innovation to develop an even greater product. Or we can seize the opportunity to expand the idea/product/service.

And when those dream stealers also attempt to steal the joy of building, let us builders pull together and invest our energy in projects/activities that create so much excitement that the staleness of the workers is completely drowned out.

# Maneuvering Around "Table-Blockers"

As we develop our brands, and make movement toward fulfilling our calls, we find ourselves invited to an array of "tables." When we are focused on authentically fulfilling our calls, our works often precede us, and our names come up in spaces we never imagined. As we take our seats at those tables, we often encounter that one person who tries to remove us from what we call the "adult table" and assign us to what we call the "kids' table." I like to call them "table-blockers."

Here are some of the tactics "table-blockers" use:

1. Refusing to acknowledge our presence. This can be evidenced by refusal to speak to us, address us by our name, or talking around us as if we do not exist.

2. Using verbal and nonverbal cues to signal that we do not belong. Sometimes this is evidenced by unwelcoming looks as if to say, "Why is *she* here?" Or they may deliver slights about our choice of attire, hairstyle, etc. Or they may emphasize accomplishments or assets they know we have not yet attained. For example, in conversation, our peers may discuss trips or assets they've purchased that we cannot yet afford. Or they might speak to appointments to committees or other positions of influence to which we have not yet gained access.

3. Invalidating our contributions and ideas through shooting them down with an unnecessary level of vitriol. Or more subtly, refuting the idea until someone else presents something similar. I could not begin to count the number of times I've been asked to participate in initiatives to solve a particular social problem. According to the leadership, I was brought on to share my experiences and successes with the issue of choice. But when the group opened up the floor for suggestions on how to move forward, and I made my suggestions, so many times my response was met with, "That cannot be done." Or I would receive looks as if to say, "That is the most ridiculous thing I've ever heard." Then someone else would give the exact same recommendation, and the

group would congratulate that person. Then they would make movement to implement the suggestion.

"Table-blockers" block for a number of reasons.

1. They want you to feel the frustration and bitterness they felt when it happened to them.

2. They are threatened by what you bring to the table.

3. They are afraid you might take their seat.

4. They have been in position so long they have forgotten that someone sacrificed for *all* of us to take our rightful seats.

Whereas we might be tempted, let us not "flip" the table over. And let us not sling "mess" across the table as they do. Instead, let us come to each and every table prepared. Here are some ways we can prepare ourselves:

1. Research who invited us and why they want us there.

2. Know who *we* are.

3. Know who *we represent.*

Once we have arrived at each table, let us:

4. Leverage who is there for *us.*

5. Engage with those who are receptive to what we have to say.

6. If we cannot find any allies, be *sure* to clearly explain who we're there to represent and be *sure* to speak up boldly for who we represent.

## QUESTIONS FOR REFLECTION

1. What tables in your work do you avoid? Or what tables do you find you must mentally and emotionally prepare for battle? Why do you avoid them, or why do you prepare for battle?

2. In what places of your work do others attempt to make you feel like you do not belong? In what ways do they attempt to make you feel like you do not belong?

3. When those situations occur, what is your most immediate reaction?

4. What strategies do you use to assert yourself and establish your right to respect?

## CLOSING

Authenticity is something no one can take from us. So there is no need to internalize or give an iota of energy to the insults we are likely to receive. Remember that people with big positions can have small minds and fragile egos and be extremely insecure. Finally, let us use every lesson learned to *create our own tables, with our own rules.* And when we create those tables, let us be sure to remember the people we represent. Let us take every opportunity to invite people who care for us, or whom we care for. Let us demonstrate the inclusivity we should all be striving for!

# Choosing Our Rings Carefully

When we are shielding ourselves from attacks continuously, we do have to remain balanced. We need to come up with a process for how we pick and choose our battles to fight. One of the temptations we must resist is stepping into rings we are not ready for.

How do we identify those rings we are not ready for? Here are a few indicators:

1. Taking up this particular fight will result in a consequence we are not ready for, i.e., loss of position, loss of resources.

2. We are not prepared professionally for the fight, as evidenced by the lack of knowledge, experience, or credentials to put forth a sound argument.

3. We are not a part of the discussion or issue. In other words, we do not have the professional authority to enter this particular ring. Nor does the fight have anything to do with our job description. Or the fight is someone else's grievance, and they are using us as their mouthpiece.

4. We are not emotionally prepared for the fight. We cannot handle the pushback we will likely receive.

## QUESTIONS FOR REFLECTION

1. When was the last time you stepped into a ring you were not ready for? What made you take on the fight in the first place? What was the outcome?

2. What are some of the ways you could have avoided that ring in the first place?

## CLOSING

As we think about how to choose our rings more carefully and how we might have stepped in the wrong ring in the past, let us examine what made such rings attractive in the first place. Was there a personal grievance involved beyond the issue at hand? Did we see an opportunity to punish someone else for an unrelated issue? Did we harbor another type of resentment about that person's position, accomplishments, or other attributes?

As female fighters, we encounter enough challenges through existing and trying to fulfill our calls. We must be careful not to complicate things by provoking people who have the power to set our lives on seriously negative paths. Furthermore, we must avoid seeking sympathy for the consequences of our own aggression. When we fight for something noble rather than fighting other people, we are much more likely to make the movement necessary to fulfill our calls. Let us not forget the bigger picture. We can grant ourselves *permission* to take a step back when we are moving toward carrying out a longer term strategy. Stepping back also shows strength, and it shows smarts. Let us fight with intentionality, strategy, and purpose!

# Prepare to Pivot

From an early age, I learned things do not always go as expected, planned, or desired.

I was taught by my dad not to expect failure but to be aware of the reality that things can go wrong. He would sit me and my baby sister down as little girls and pace back and forth with different questions: "What if __ happens?" Then he'd turn around and point to one of us to answer. I'm not going to say he didn't help refine the answer, but he always challenged us to think first.

Sometimes in these situations it's a natural mishap, but we must grant ourselves *permission* to anticipate and prepare for the reality of sabotage. For example, I have had speeches stolen from me, microphones tampered with, displays destroyed, lies told, and attempts to steal my projects and ideas. I have had groups infiltrated, controversies created, and many other experiences sabotaged. Whereas I wish I could say these events only began in my adulthood, I learned the reality of sabotage very early in my childhood.

And then, at other times, mishaps occur because of negligence and lack of competence. Believe it or not, paid professionals can and do drop balls that they should not. Paid professionals do overextend themselves sometimes and take on more business than they can handle competently. If we are one of the lower-paying clients, sometimes our jobs are neglected. Sometimes, simply because we're women, paid professionals do not give us the same quality of work. Why? Because they expect us to grin and bear it.

## QUESTIONS FOR REFLECTION

1. Can you think of any experiences you have had when you were required to take the lead on a project, and someone else's sabotage or negligence left you exposed? Was it negligence or sabotage? When the sabotage or negligence occurred, how did you handle it in the moment?

2. Are you still required to work with those people who initiated the sabotage or negligence? If you are not required to, do you still work with these people? Why or why not?

3. What lessons did you learn from the situation? In what ways do you now anticipate potential sabotage and negligence? How do you prepare to pivot?

## CLOSING

As we've discussed, we need not become fixated with the realities of sabotage or negligence. As we acknowledge them, we can develop solutions ahead of time. We figure out how we can pivot and adjust. We develop ways to transform vulnerabilities into strength.

Here are a few strategies we can use to prepare for mishaps and potential sabotage:

1. Have a backup when possible (two copies of speeches, time stamps, copyrighting of material before submission).

2. Where possible, bring our own equipment. If supplying equipment is not possible, then schedule time beforehand to test the equipment. Ask questions about the equipment specifications. And if we have someone we trust, allow them to negotiate these details on our behalf.

3. Where graciously possible, give ourselves *permission* to call out the sabotage or lack of competency. For example, if we are giving a presentation and our microphone or AV equipment is not set up properly, it is okay to stop, pause, and request the issue be fixed before moving on.

4. If we encounter issues during a public speech or performance, it is okay to start over and re-establish our rhythms.

5. When we are presenting a new idea, it is okay to keep at least some of the information to ourselves, or find an alternate form of delivering the information. That way, saboteurs can't steal everything, and we leave room for the pivot or adjustment.

In other words, let us be prepared to make lemonade out of lemons!

# Moving to Greener Pastures

If we intend to overcome, we must also give ourselves *permission* to look for and seize new opportunities. Unfortunately, as women, we still live and work in a world where too many people are still only comfortable with *leveraging* our gifts and expertise. Many people are not yet comfortable with women *leading* with their gifts and expertise. Nor are they comfortable *learning* from the women who possess those gifts and expertise. This discomfort is evidenced by a number of toxic behaviors that lead to a cultural gravitational pull, which resists growth, kills aspirations, and leads to a failure to strive and soar. Instilling the principle of seeking and seizing new opportunities provides a buffer against that gravitational pull. *Permission* to look for and seize new opportunities inspires us to persist and break free so we can fulfill our calls!

One indicator that may signal it is time to move to greener pastures is persistent bullying from those who are supposed to share similar values, missions, and goals. This is often evidenced by consistent exposure to nonverbal and verbal gestures (smacked lips, rolling eyes, nasty muttering under the breath), plus being insulted by the same people most likely to benefit from our contributions. Other bullying tactics include a refusal to acknowledge or appreciate our contributions, as well as reducing our contributions to acts of personal servitude. Other tactics include taking projects we've developed and assigning them to others to take credit for the foundational work we've done. Sometimes this bullying is also evidenced through stripping our budgets of necessary resources, forcing us to do more with less, while those resources are allocated to others who have not made as many or as significant contributions. Finally, this bullying can be evidenced through frivolous and inequitable disciplinary action to damage our records, and to further make us feel hopeless and inadequate.

When this sort of bullying continues to occur, it is often a sign that this is a table where we do not belong. When the same people who benefit from our expertise and gifts resent us for contributing our expertise and gifts, this is an indicator of a strong resentment. Oftentimes, resentment may stem from people who envy our ability to authentically answer, accept, and make steps to fulfill our calls. Many times, they are still listening for theirs and haven't made any progress because they were trying to accept someone else's call instead of their own.

Though we lead with love, graciousness, and humility, there are times when we must set boundaries. Other people's baggage cannot become our baggage. When we stay in a situation or a position too long, we begin to internalize the bullying we have experienced. We run the risk of stifling our gifts, killing our dreams, and losing the drive to fulfill our calls. We can also become bitter and become bullies ourselves, killing the dreams and aspirations of those coming behind us.

## QUESTIONS FOR REFLECTION

1. What indicators do you use to determine if it is time to move to greener pastures?

2. How satisfied are you in your current professional role? Do you believe your current professional role is granting you the space to fulfill your call?

3. What is the culture and climate at your current place of employment? Are you bullied? If you do believe you are

bullied, why do you stay? Are there other spaces in your life where you are bullied? Why do you stay?

4. When was the last time you did research on the demand specific to your profession? To what degree are you aware of options to move to greener pastures? If you are not aware and are not doing research, why is that?

## CLOSING

When we give ourselves *permission* to seek and to move to greener pastures, we open our eyes to new possibilities. But we also empower ourselves to act more assertively in our present situations. It is easier to speak up and advocate for ourselves when we do not believe we must stay stuck where we are. Remember, openness to change is essential. For if we do not move forward, we will fall backward.

# Play to Win

In order to overcome obstacles to fulfilling our calls, we must give ourselves *permission* to play to win! The world will keep turning. People will keep achieving. And the organizations we are leading will continue to move in the direction that promotes success and sustainability. The question is, Do we want to be a part of the success, be left behind in the success, or be run over by the success?

Oftentimes as women, we are conditioned to graciously concede what belongs to us. We are told to contribute winning products but deny our involvement. We are often pressured to hand the credit to someone else, who then co-opts our innovation and efforts for their own. When we continue to "graciously concede," we often nurse resentment underneath. And resentment is often directed toward unassuming individuals (most times other women), who play to win within the bounds of ethics. The resentment often emerges because there is a regret for not having the courage to play to win. And the woman who dares to win brings that regret to the surface. How do we recondition ourselves? One way is through surrounding ourselves with people who affirm our permission to play to win!

**The question is, Do we want to be a part of the success, be left behind in the success, or be run over by the success?**

I have a couple of memories to share that gave me *permission* to play to win. My father was recruited to coach my softball team based on my growth in the previous year. He took a team who had a losing season the year before and coached them all the way to the championship.

I remember we were down in the last inning, with two players on base. Back then, I did not meet BMI standards, and for that reason, plus my swing, I batted clean-up. Those attributes made for a great hitter but were not necessarily society's most desirable traits for a thirteen-year-old girl. On my way from the batter's box to the plate, my dad whispers in my ear, "When you get up there, knock the *hell* out of that ball!" And that's exactly what I did. I cleared those bases with what people said was one of the longest triples in history (LOL, I never could run), and won the championship for my team!

Fast forward twenty-five years. It was 2018, and my organization, Center of Hope, was in the running for a state and local award for enrichment and innovation. In so many ways, 2018 was a tumultuous time. I saw the lengths people went to, people who are paid to serve our children, people who said they had the same struggles as our children, to try to *stop* us from doing the work we were qualified to do—the work at which we had excelled for so many years! We were threatened. We were locked out of buildings. Our property was destroyed. I was physically shoved on several occasions. Fingers were pointed in my face, as well as other forms of intimidation. At the time, I did not feel led to move on to greener pastures because the children and families we educated and served were depending on us. We had signed contracts to provide services to them, and we were not going to let them down.

My father, no longer my "formal" coach but who will probably always see himself fulfilling that role, said, "Every time they hit you, hit back harder!" He also said, "The more they attack you, the more you multiply!" And that's what we did. For every slight, we put more time and focus into helping our children learn and excel. For every act of intimidation, we offered more responsive services to our families. And as a result, we won both distinctions: State champions for literacy and the Local Excellence and Innovation Award winners.

Another way we can play to win is by taking satisfaction in following through. We play to win when we do what we set out to accomplish. When we have an expectation of success, we may not always be the first one recruited into a social circle. Some people, whether they admit it or not, are often concerned about one person's light dimming someone else's light. Or they are concerned that one person's high expectations will upset the comfortability of the "status quo." There are some people who see social interactions as competing lights. It is unfortunate, but an opportunity is still apparent. When we are unapologetically ourselves, and we enter spaces with the intent to uplift ourselves and others, there are times where we can shift the atmosphere. Sometimes, we can transform the atmosphere from competing lights to a garden of many colors.

## QUESTIONS FOR REFLECTION

1. In what areas/spaces have you been told directly or indirectly not to play to win? Who benefits from you not playing to win?

2. When you play to win, who supports you and who does not?

3. In what ways can you return a "hit" with a harder hit that establishes your right to own your wins?

4. Are you more likely to see social interactions as competing lights or a garden of many colors? Why?

5. In what ways can you affirm other women playing to *win*?

## CLOSING

Let us continue to reinforce that it is okay to *win*! We must refuse to hold back on our gifts or expressions to suit or pacify anyone else. We must reverse society's tendency to punish women for excelling and refuse to participate in it. We must reject the notion of relationship building as it results in everyone coming to the experience watered-down, with their gifts buried. We must resist applauding, uplifting, and continuously giving platforms to those who intentionally choose mediocrity.

And when we play to win, we can also play to help others *win*. In my case, I *win* when I give children and adults the opportunities to avoid involvement in the justice system through providing meaningful diversion alternatives. I *win* when I provide opportunities for adults to obtain decent-paying jobs.

So, to those of us who have a gift/call burning inside that we are afraid to unleash because of resistance or ridicule, it's time we give ourselves *permission* to *win*. We cannot make progress in our lives, or in our society through bending to pressure from those who do not have our best interest at heart. Let us treat our talents, our ideas, our work, our intellectual property as the valuable games they are. Let us fight until we are compensated equitably! Let us expand our lens beyond solely rallying around what we don't have—assuming we must settle for the size of the pie we currently have. Instead, let us open our minds so we can fight for a larger pie and more pies! Let us open our minds to rallying around how we can expand the pie, where we can all have some of that pie, and we can even increase what we have. Though sometimes our wins will come in increments, *we will win*!

# Key Points to Remember

- We have the capacity to define femininity for ourselves. We should reject any notion that suggests that as women, we should not fight for our calls, fight for ourselves, or fight for the elevation of others.

- We should protect our intellectual property from imitators to the best of our ability, but also let their tendencies to imitate be our motivation to continue to create, and always stay on the cutting-edge.

- As we are excluded from tables, let us give ourselves *permission* to create new tables. But in doing so, let us make sure we lead with love and inclusivity.

- Whereas we give ourselves permission to fight, let it not be our immediate reaction to do so. Let us fight with intentionality and purpose.

- We should continue to anticipate the unexpected without allowing the unexpected to erode our confidence. Instead, let us proactively develop opportunities to pivot.

- Let us proactively stay informed of opportunities to grow, explore, and expand, so we do not remain stuck. Let us also remain open to greener pastures so we operate from a place of power in our current situations.

- Let us give ourselves and others permission to *win*!

# Elevation in Action

As we leave this chapter, I have a few challenges that will support your desire to fight and win with a purpose.

1. List those who you believe are a threat to your innovation, leadership, or projects. Name three strategies you can explore to keep your ideas, approaches, and projects on the cutting edge.

2. Make a list of three strategies you can use to multiply your efforts and performance when you are attacked by internal and external threats.

3. Make a list of the fights in your professional spaces that you should take up for the purpose of principle and describe how you can ensure you are personally and professionally prepared for such fights.

4. Research the demand and pay scale for your current position, as well as any positions you would like to elevate into. Do you see any opportunities to expand or explore? Make a list of strategies you can explore to develop yourself for a new opportunity if your organization is giving you indications that it might be time to move on.

5. Make a list of three ways you can amplify your wins, along with three ways you can amplify the wins of other women.

# Now Let Us Overcome!

As we close out these chapters and reinforce the beauty and value of feminine fighters, I want to leave you with a poem I hope encourages you on those difficult, challenging days. Let us remember: We are enough. We are amazing. We are fighters, and we are overcomers. As we conclude this book, let us walk away energized, empowered, and ready! The title of this poem is "Now Let Us Overcome!"

*I think for myself.*

*I speak for myself.*

*I am strong.*

*I have a calling to fulfill, and I will fulfill it.*

*I am a fighter. I am an overcomer.*

*I will overcome!*

*I have gifts. They are mine to share.*

*I have a call. I will fulfill it. I am not scared.*

*I have a calling to fulfill, and I will fulfill it.*

*I am a fighter. I am an overcomer.*

*I will overcome!*

*I will operate in excellence.*

*I will create with conscientiousness.*

*I will not compromise my wellness.*

*I have a calling to fulfill, and I will fulfill it.*

*I am a fighter. I am an overcomer.*

*I will overcome!*

*When you see me, you may not see my scars.*

*You may not see my tears, and you may not feel my pain.*

*That's okay because each disappointment and pain will lead to my ultimate gain.*

*I have a calling to fulfill, and I will fulfill it.*

*I am a fighter. I am an overcomer.*

*I will overcome!*

*I will not succeed and turn my back.*

*I will step to centerstage, leading, loving, offering an alternative track.*

*To those who feel shut out, discouraged, dreams stagnant, emotions out of whack.*

*They have a calling to fulfill, and they can fulfill it.*

*They are fighters. They are overcomers!*

*They will overcome!*

*Let us set aside every comparison, every hurt.*

*Leading with love, loving with discernment.*

*Taking new risks, opening new doors.*

*Let us unleash the stories of our sisters—they need to be heard.*

*We have callings to fulfill, and we will fulfill them.*

*We are fighters. We are overcomers!*

*Now let us overcome!*

# ELEVATING GROWTH

We have been on quite a journey—exploring ourselves, exploring how we present and represent ourselves, exploring how we maneuver in settings that do not necessarily appreciate who or what we represent. But we've also explored how we resist the temptation to become bitter and resentful in the face of adversity. We continue to approach situations with love and understanding, while fighting for principles and people when it is warranted.

As we close out this book and this journey of exploration, let us grant ourselves one last *permission: permission* to *grow*! Giving ourselves permission to grow is so essential because we often live and work in a world where we as women are pressured to be perfect,

> Giving ourselves permission to grow is so essential because we often live and work in a world where we as women are pressured to be perfect, though perfection is impossible.

though perfection is impossible. Giving ourselves permission to grow helps us reject such pressure. Giving ourselves permission to grow allows us to see opportunities and lessons in the challenges we face. That way, we can enjoy the process of building, navigating, loving, and overcoming.

So, as we move forward, applying the lessons presented in this book, let us give ourselves at least these four permissions related to growth:

1. Permission to grow from our experiences. When we give ourselves permission to grow from our experiences, we recognize we can only make decisions with the information we have in the moment. We understand we can be thrown into situations we have not had the training and experience to navigate. We understand when we are capable, we are often thrown into challenges no one else knows how to handle or cares to handle. When we give ourselves permission to grow from our experiences, we demonstrate we can analyze ambiguities and complexities within situations. If it were easy, then anyone could solve the problem! If the problem could be solved without critical self-reflection, refinement, and adjustment, then anyone would attempt to solve the problem. When we give ourselves permission to grow from our experiences, we see tasks and situations as a part of an entire journey, rather than a checklist of items by which we can please others. And, when we let go of the desire to please others and appear perfect, our liberation to fulfill our calls begins.

2. Permission to grow into experiences. When we give ourselves permission to grow into experiences, we understand that life will throw us curve balls. We recognize there are some

experiences we cannot prepare for. Whereas we prepare to the best of our ability, we also know that moving to greener pastures will often require us to move out of our comfort zones. Seizing new opportunities will challenge and stretch our capacities. When we give ourselves permission to grow into experiences, we are more poised to take calculated risks. And in doing so, we open our lives to much richer and greater possibilities. The reality is for most of us, our call is not clear. We usually do not know exactly what the outcome will be. But when we are not encumbered by fears of inadequacy, our trajectories are much greater.

3. Permission to grow with others. When we lead with love, humility, and gratitude, we are able to share our journeys with others. When we are sensitive to the struggles of others, we are more transparent about our own struggles. And this sets the stage for an amazing support system of people who can grow together. When we find people who are kind and looking for nothing in return, and they are transparent, authentic, and have the capacity to hold us accountable, those are the types of people we need to keep in our inner circles. In dialogue, we have the capacity to learn from their struggles. We can find validation for the struggles we have already encountered. And we can learn from others which paths to pursue and which paths to avoid.

4. Permission to grow beyond others. When we elevate growth, it often becomes apparent who wants to grow with you and who does not. Whereas we do not have to share the same aspirations, openness to new experiences is essential for leadership. Rigidity can stagnate our growth as leaders. It

is one thing to stand on principles and refuse to budge. But we need to make sure we are not surrounding ourselves with people who refuse to budge on their preferences. When we spend too much time around people who have no desire to grow, we run the risk of being left behind ourselves. We must grant ourselves permission to change circles unapologetically when we find ourselves in spaces where the same projects, the same discourse, and the same goals are the focus for prolonged periods of time. And we must grow into a new circle, particularly when we find ourselves in a space where the narrative revolves around "why we can't" more than "how we will."

As I close out this book, I would like to leave you with one last poem I wrote, called "Grow." On those days we feel our decisions and actions did not measure up, let us remind ourselves that falling short is a part of the growth process. When we feel we are excelling, it is my hope that this poem is a reminder to identify, seek, and assume a new challenge!

# Grow

*It is my hope that I am not who I was yesterday, and that tomorrow, I will not be who I am today.*

*I must grow!*

*I will not feel guilty about the choices of today, believing I led with the knowledge, skills, and resources I had in place.*

*There is always room to grow!*

*I will kick barriers out of my way, while I will pray and seek direction as not to stray.*

*So I can continue to grow!*

*I will break every oppressive chain, for the next group of women leaders on the way!*

*I will help them grow!*

*I will press forward in hope, looking for every opportunity to learn, knowing all this effort will lead to a brighter day!*

*With the light we create, the light we facilitate, and the light we shine, we can, we must, we will grow!*

# ACKNOWLEDGMENTS

I would like to thank Faris Alami, my mentor from the Goldman Sachs 10,000 Small Businesses program. He was the first to encourage me to write about my professional journey. Thank you to my childhood friend, Courtney Stith, for encouraging me to write this particular book. Thank you to my baby sister, Dr. Staci Perryman-Clark, whose pains from seeking to do trailblazing work inspired my desire to provide words of hope and healing. Thank you to two instrumental women during my high school years, Mrs. Christine Rode and Mrs. Jane Charette. Thank you, Mrs. Rode, for challenging me from the day I walked into St. Ursula Academy, and encouraging me to think and write about equity and justice. Thank you to my favorite principal, Mrs. Jane Charette, for giving me my first opportunities to lead and amplify my voice. Thank you to my mentors, Sarah Skow and Patricia Wise, who have helped me refine and expand my approach to leadership, and who have helped me prepare my organization to grow exponentially!

# ABOUT THE AUTHOR

Tracee Perryman, PhD, is CEO and co-founder of Center of Hope Family Services, where she has developed evidence-based programming for positive youth development that empowers families and communities. The organization's successes have established Dr. Perryman as a recognized expert in achieving positive life outcomes for individuals often labeled as at-risk by employing data-driven, evidence-based interventions that are culturally relevant. A sought-after speaker, presenter, and performer, she brings expertise on innovative approaches in afterschool education and family empowerment.

Dr. Perryman is the author of the books *Elevating Futures: A Model for Empowering Black Elementary Student Success* and *ELEVATE! An Afterschool Enrichment Curriculum for Fostering Children's Academic, Social and Emotional Resilience*. Dr. Perryman is the creator of ELEVATE!, a recognized multicultural K–3 afterschool program that increases confidence, improves social and emotional skills, and elevates academic performance for underserved children in urban and suburban communities. The ELEVATE! Learning Management Software, set for release in the fall of 2023, will empower school systems across the country to implement this award-winning education model in their communities.

Dr. Perryman lives and works in Toledo, Ohio.

Printed in the USA
CPSIA information can be obtained
at www.ICGtesting.com
JSHW021436161023
50269JS00007B/67